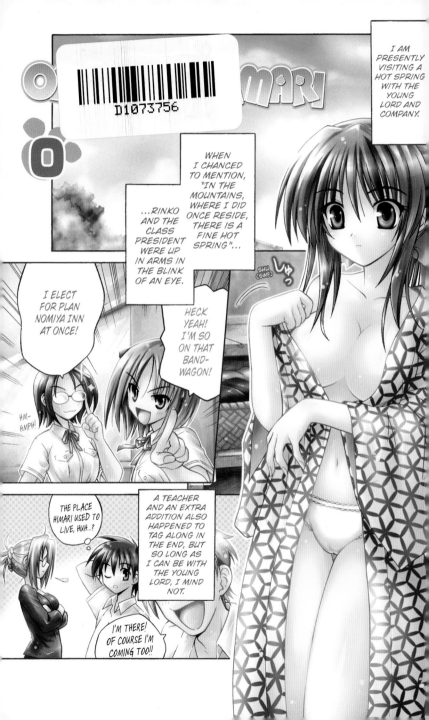

I AM PRESENTLY VISITING A HOT SPRING WITH THE YOUNG LORD AND COMPANY.

WHEN I CHANCED TO MENTION, "IN THE MOUNTAINS, WHERE I DID ONCE RESIDE, THERE IS A FINE HOT SPRING"...

...RINKO AND THE CLASS PRESIDENT WERE UP IN ARMS IN THE BLINK OF AN EYE.

SHU (SWF)

I ELECT FOR PLAN NOMIYA INN AT ONCE!

HECK YEAH! I'M SO ON THAT BAND-WAGON!

HM-HMPH!

THE PLACE HIMARI USED TO LIVE, HUH...?

A TEACHER AND AN EXTRA ADDITION ALSO HAPPENED TO TAG ALONG IN THE END, BUT SO LONG AS I CAN BE WITH THE YOUNG LORD, I MIND NOT.

I'M THERE! OF COURSE I'M COMING TOO!!

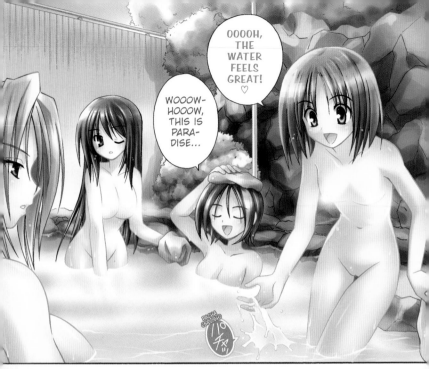

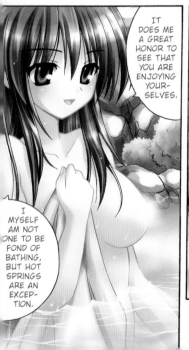

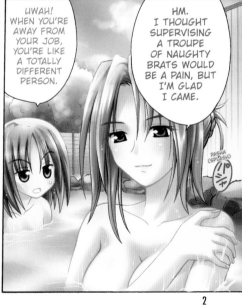

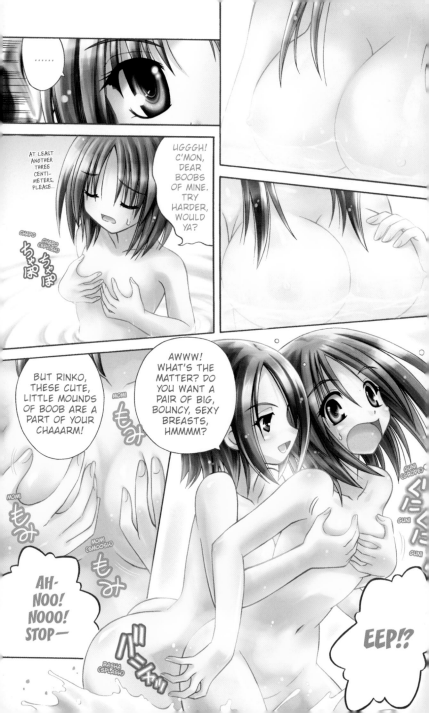

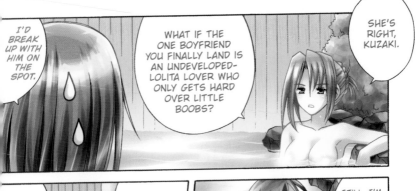

I'D BREAK UP WITH HIM ON THE SPOT.

WHAT IF THE ONE BOYFRIEND YOU FINALLY LAND IS AN UNDEVELOPED-LOLITA LOVER WHO ONLY GETS HARD OVER LITTLE BOOBS?

SHE'S RIGHT, KUZAKI.

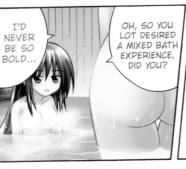

I'D NEVER BE SO BOLD...

OH, SO YOU LOT DESIRED A MIXED BATH EXPERIENCE, DID YOU?

FOR REAL! NOT ONLY ARE WE ALL HOT GIRLS, BUT THERE'S FOUR OF US.

STILL, I'M SURPRISED THE BOYS HAVEN'T SNUCK OVER TO SPY ON US.

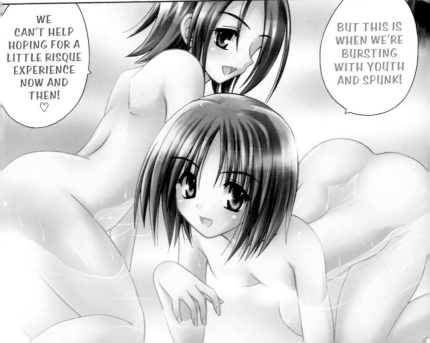

WE CAN'T HELP HOPING FOR A LITTLE RISQUE EXPERIENCE NOW AND THEN! ♡

BUT THIS IS WHEN WE'RE BURSTING WITH YOUTH AND SPUNK!

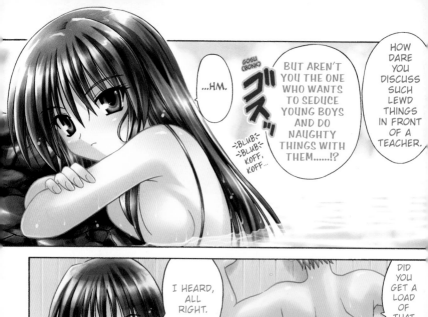
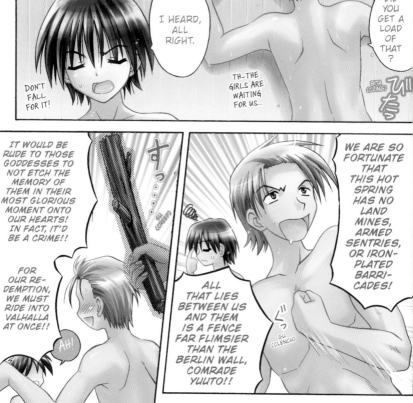

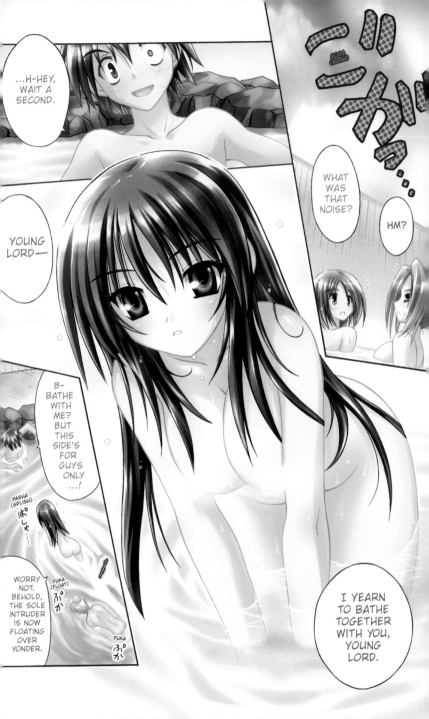

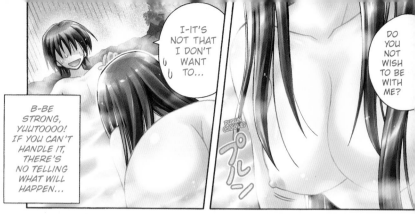

I-IT'S NOT THAT I DON'T WANT TO...

DO YOU NOT WISH TO BE WITH ME?

B-BE STRONG, YUUTOOOO! IF YOU CAN'T HANDLE IT, THERE'S NO TELLING WHAT WILL HAPPEN...

プルーン

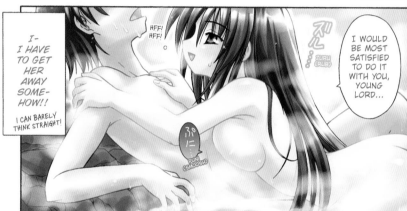

I- I HAVE TO GET HER AWAY SOMEHOW!! I CAN BARELY THINK STRAIGHT!

HFF! HFF!

ズル

I WOULD BE MOST SATISFIED TO DO IT WITH YOU, YOUNG LORD...

ぷに

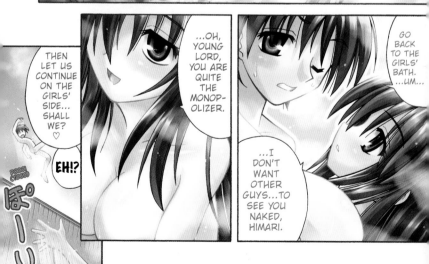

THEN LET US CONTINUE ON THE GIRLS' SIDE... SHALL WE? ♡

EH!?

ぽーーーん

...OH, YOUNG LORD, YOU ARE QUITE THE MONOPOLIZER.

GO BACK TO THE GIRLS' BATH. ...UM...

...I DON'T WANT OTHER GUYS...TO SEE YOU NAKED, HIMARI.

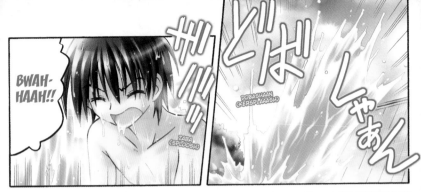

BWAH-HAAH!!

ザバ
(SPLOOSH)

どばしゃあん
DOBASHAAN
(K'ERSPLAAASH)

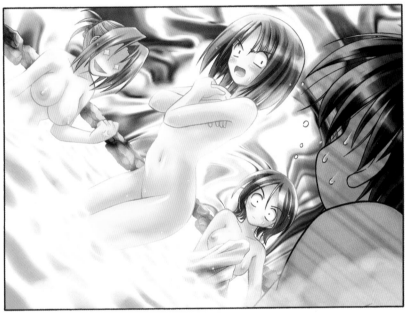

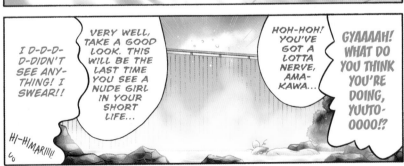

I D-D-D-D-DIDN'T SEE ANY-THING! I SWEAR!!

HI-HIMARI!!!!!

VERY WELL, TAKE A GOOD LOOK. THIS WILL BE THE LAST TIME YOU SEE A NUDE GIRL IN YOUR SHORT LIFE...

HOH-HOH! YOU'VE GOT A LOTTA NERVE, AMA-KAWA...

GYAAAAH! WHAT DO YOU THINK YOU'RE DOING, YUUTO-OOOO!?

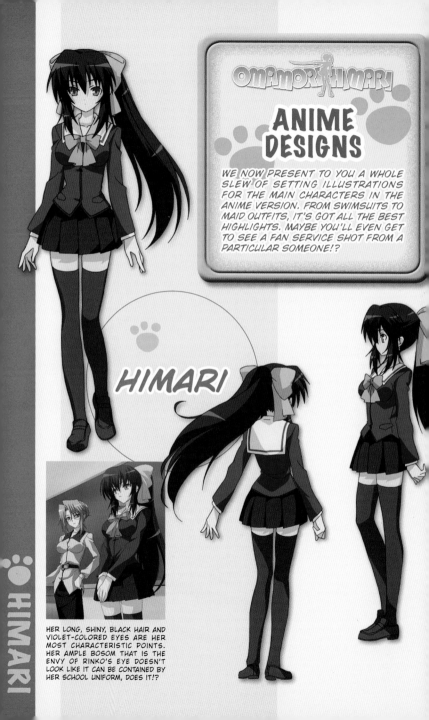

OMAMORI HIMARI

ANIME DESIGNS

WE NOW PRESENT TO YOU A WHOLE SLEW OF SETTING ILLUSTRATIONS FOR THE MAIN CHARACTERS IN THE ANIME VERSION. FROM SWIMSUITS TO MAID OUTFITS, IT'S GOT ALL THE BEST HIGHLIGHTS. MAYBE YOU'LL EVEN GET TO SEE A FAN SERVICE SHOT FROM A PARTICULAR SOMEONE!?

HIMARI

HER LONG, SHINY, BLACK HAIR AND VIOLET-COLORED EYES ARE HER MOST CHARACTERISTIC POINTS. HER AMPLE BOSOM THAT IS THE ENVY OF RINKO'S EYE DOESN'T LOOK LIKE IT CAN BE CONTAINED BY HER SCHOOL UNIFORM, DOES IT!?

HIMARI

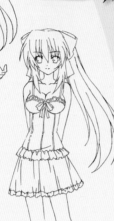

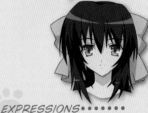

EXPRESSIONS········

PART OF WHAT MAKES HIMARI SO ENDEARING IS HER RANGE OF FACIAL EXPRESSIONS. YET WHY IS IT SHE ONLY BLUSHES WHEN IT COMES TO YUUTO...?

CLOTHING ·········

FROM THE HAIR TIE SHE WEARS WHEN SHE'S IN A BATHING SUIT TO THE CASUAL ATTIRE YUUTO BOUGHT HER, ALL OF HIMARI'S OUTFITS WILL BE RECREATED FOR THE ANIME, DOWN TO THE FINEST DETAILS. UNDER HER CAT-EAR MAID SKIRT, SHE EVEN WEARS A SEXY LITTLE GARTER BELT.

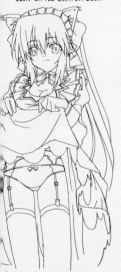

YASUTSUNA

THE KATANA HIMARI REQUIRES WHEN BATTLING AYAKASHI. IN THE ANIME AS WELL, THIS SWORD WILL BE A CONSTANT COMPANION OF HIMARI'S AS SHE PROTECTS YUUTO.

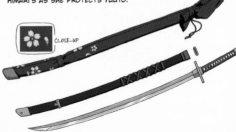

CLOSE-UP

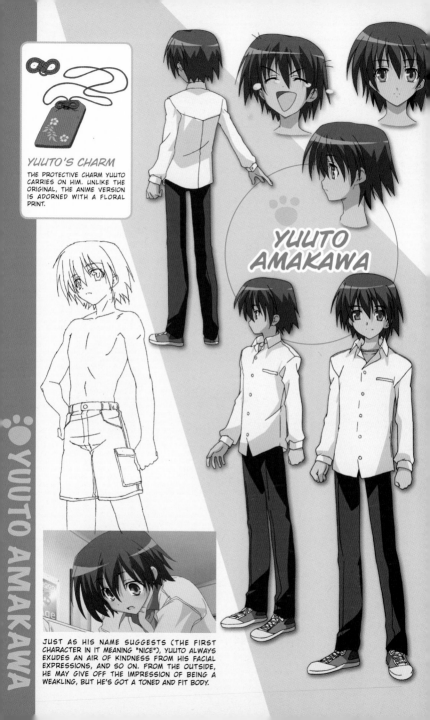

YUUTO'S CHARM

THE PROTECTIVE CHARM YUUTO CARRIES ON HIM. UNLIKE THE ORIGINAL, THE ANIME VERSION IS ADORNED WITH A FLORAL PRINT.

YUUTO AMAKAWA

JUST AS HIS NAME SUGGESTS (THE FIRST CHARACTER IN IT MEANING "NICE"), YUUTO ALWAYS EXUDES AN AIR OF KINDNESS FROM HIS FACIAL EXPRESSIONS, AND SO ON. FROM THE OUTSIDE, HE MAY GIVE OFF THE IMPRESSION OF BEING A WEAKLING, BUT HE'S GOT A TONED AND FIT BODY.

YUUTO AMAKAWA

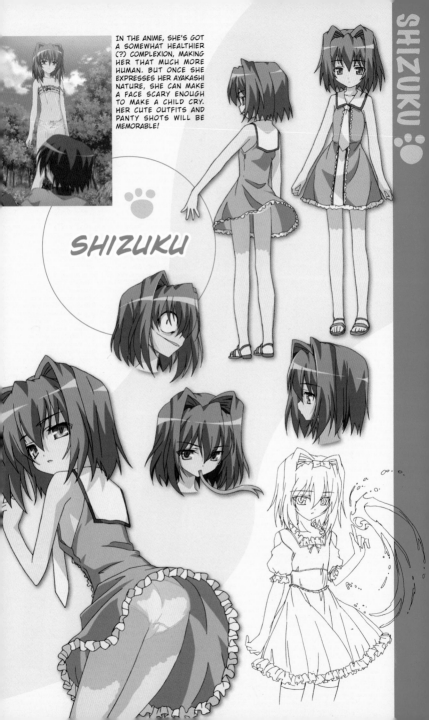

IN THE ANIME, SHE'S GOT A SOMEWHAT HEALTHIER (?) COMPLEXION, MAKING HER THAT MUCH MORE HUMAN. BUT ONCE SHE EXPRESSES HER AYAKASHI NATURE, SHE CAN MAKE A FACE SCARY ENOUGH TO MAKE A CHILD CRY. HER CUTE OUTFITS AND PANTY SHOTS WILL BE MEMORABLE!

SHIZUKU

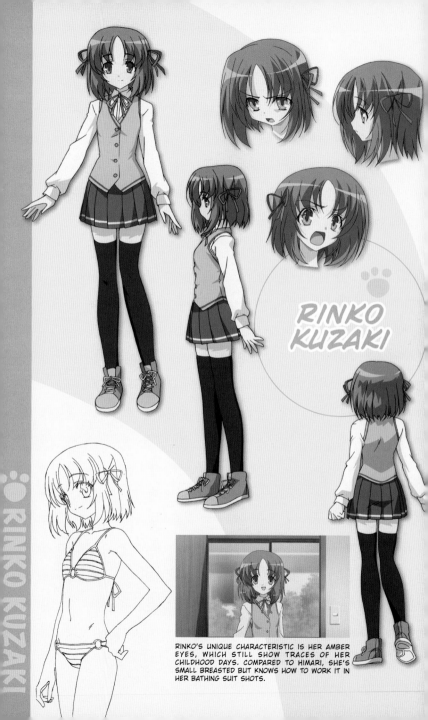

RINKO
KUZAKI

RINKO'S UNIQUE CHARACTERISTIC IS HER AMBER
EYES, WHICH STILL SHOW TRACES OF HER
CHILDHOOD DAYS. COMPARED TO HIMARI, SHE'S
SMALL BREASTED BUT KNOWS HOW TO WORK IT IN
HER BATHING SUIT SHOTS.

RINKO KUZAKI

LIZLET L. CHELSIE

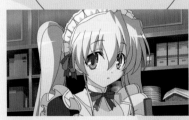

DESPITE ALL THE FRILLS ON HER MAID UNIFORM, HER CLEAVAGE IS STILL AS EYE-CATCHING AS EVER. AND HER STREAMING, GOLDEN PIGTAILS ARE SURE TO BE LOVELY!

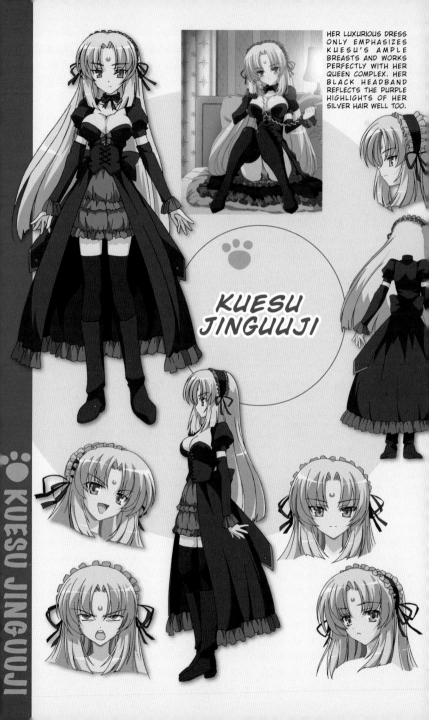

HER LUXURIOUS DRESS ONLY EMPHASIZES KUESU'S AMPLE BREASTS AND WORKS PERFECTLY WITH HER QUEEN COMPLEX. HER BLACK HEADBAND REFLECTS THE PURPLE HIGHLIGHTS OF HER SILVER HAIR WELL TOO.

KUESU JINGUUJI

KUESU JINGUUJI

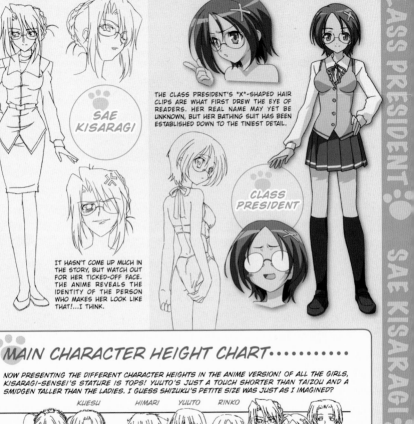

SAE KISARAGI

CLASS PRESIDENT

THE CLASS PRESIDENT'S "X"-SHAPED HAIR CLIPS ARE WHAT FIRST DREW THE EYE OF READERS. HER REAL NAME MAY YET BE UNKNOWN, BUT HER BATHING SUIT HAS BEEN ESTABLISHED DOWN TO THE TINIEST DETAIL.

IT HASN'T COME UP MUCH IN THE STORY, BUT WATCH OUT FOR HER TICKED-OFF FACE. THE ANIME REVEALS THE IDENTITY OF THE PERSON WHO MAKES HER LOOK LIKE THAT!...I THINK.

MAIN CHARACTER HEIGHT CHART · · · · · · · · · · ·

NOW PRESENTING THE DIFFERENT CHARACTER HEIGHTS IN THE ANIME VERSION! OF ALL THE GIRLS, KISARAGI-SENSEI'S STATURE IS TOPS! YUUTO'S JUST A TOUCH SHORTER THAN TAIZOU AND A SMIDGEN TALLER THAN THE LADIES. I GUESS SHIZUKU'S PETITE SIZE WAS JUST AS I IMAGINED?

KUESU · · · HIMARI · · · YUUTO · · · RINKO

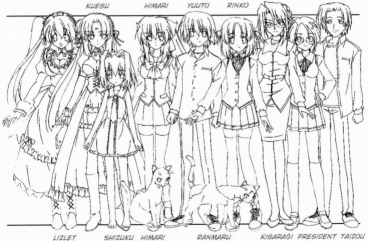

LIZLET · · · · · SHIZUKU · HIMARI (CAT) · · · · · RANMARU · · · · · KISARAGI · PRESIDENT · TAIZOU

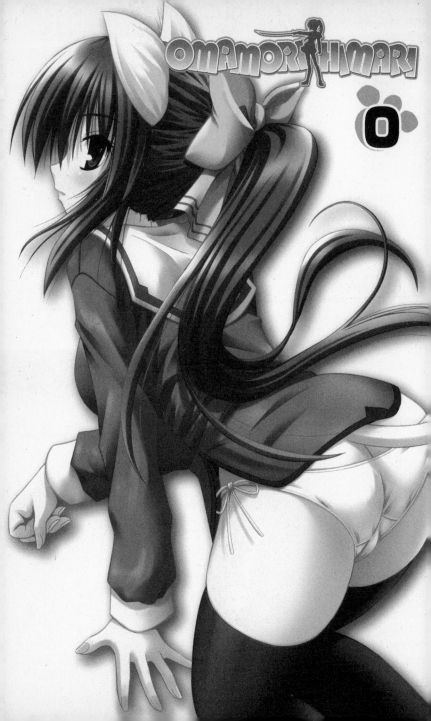

CONTENTS

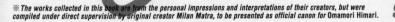

※ *The works collected in this book are from the personal impressions and interpretations of their creators, but were compiled under direct supervision by original creator Milan Matra, to be presented as official canon for Omamori Himari.*

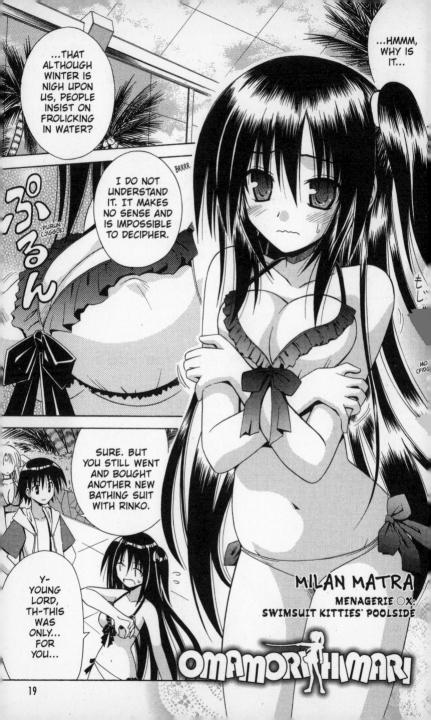

...THAT ALTHOUGH WINTER IS NIGH UPON US, PEOPLE INSIST ON FROLICKING IN WATER?

...HMMM, WHY IS IT...

I DO NOT UNDERSTAND IT. IT MAKES NO SENSE AND IS IMPOSSIBLE TO DECIPHER.

BRRRR.

ぷ〜ん
PURUN
(JIGGLE)

SURE. BUT YOU STILL WENT AND BOUGHT ANOTHER NEW BATHING SUIT WITH RINKO.

Y-YOUNG LORD, TH-THIS WAS ONLY... FOR YOU...

MILAN MATRA
MENAGERIE ◯X:
SWIMSUIT KITTIES' POOLSIDE

OMAMORI HIMARI

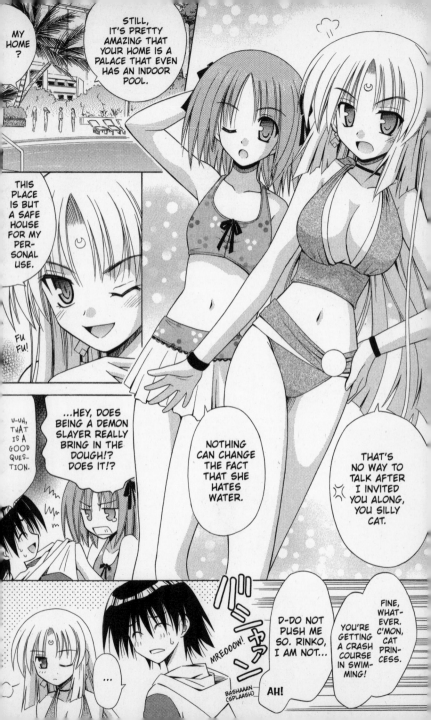

YOU PROBABLY PACK YOUR BUST WITH TEA LEAVES, DON'T YOU!?

B-BREAST SIZE ISN'T EVERYTHING, I'LL HAVE YOU KNOW!!

BISHI (JAB)

WHAAAT?

I USED EARL GREY AS A BASE AND THEN ADDED FLAVORS LIKE MANGO, PASSION FRUIT, AND ROSE FLOWERS.

YUUTO-SAN LOVE, LOVE, LOOOOVES MY MOUNDS OF JOY!

HOW RUDE. AND YOU, KUESU-SAN, PROBABLY ENLARGE YOUR BREASTS WITH MAGIC, HMM?

POYON. (BOUNCE)

TAKE THAT!

MUNI (SQUISH)

AND FOR THE RECORD, MY BOSOM'S THE BIGGEST! ♡

AH, AYA-SAN.

MY, YOU ARE RATHER POPU-LAR.

YUUTO-SAMA.

I'LL NOT HAVE THE LIKES OF SOME ROTTEN WITCH TAKE THAT TONE WITH ME!

=DROOP=

WHAT DID YOU SAY, YOU SLUTTY MAID!!?

22

HERE, FOR EXAMPLE... IT IS SURE TO BECOME TRANSPARENT. IT REALLY IS QUITE A SIGHT.

ゆさっ
YUSA
(STROKE)

YUUTO-SAMA, AS YOU KNOW, MY BODY IS MADE OF PAPER.

...WOULD YOU NOT CARE TO OBSERVE?

R-RIGHT.

UH! AH! Y-YES.

HER SKIN'S SO WHITE.

どか
DOKA
(WHACK)

ドボーン
DOBOON
(SPLOSH)

SO IF I AM DAMPENED WITH WATER, I BECOME RUMPLED AND SOPPING WET.

SOP-PING... WET?

BASHAA
(SPLASH)

ばしゃあ

TEE-HEE. THAT YUUTO-SAMA IS MOST AMUSING.

HEE!

HEE!

=BLUB=
=BLUB=
=BLUB=

D-ROOOWN!!

SHE MAY HAVE A PRETTY FACE, BUT SHE'S JUST SOME FANCY ORIGAMI WORK!! YOU GET ME!?

HOW CAN YOU GET ALL SLACK-JAWED OVER SOME PAD OF PAPER!?

THE END

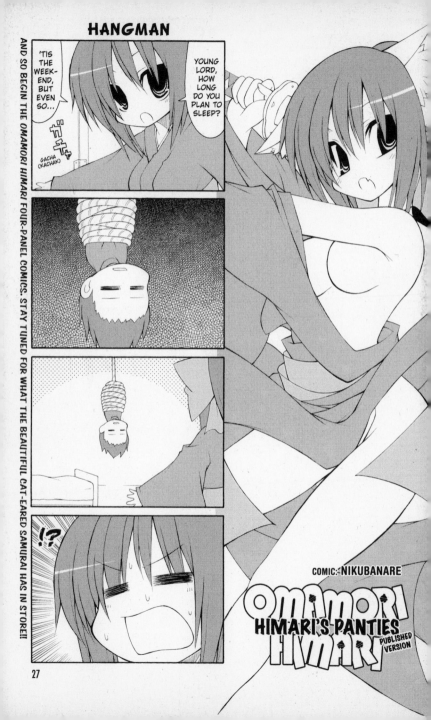

EASY

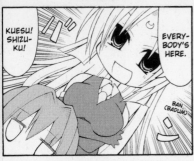

KUESU! SHIZU-KU!

EVERY-BODY'S HERE.

BAN (BADUH)

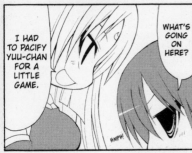

I HAD TO PACIFY YUU-CHAN FOR A LITTLE GAME.

WHAT'S GOING ON HERE?

HMPH!

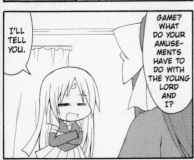

I'LL TELL YOU.

GAME? WHAT DO YOUR AMUSE-MENTS HAVE TO DO WITH THE YOUNG LORD AND I?

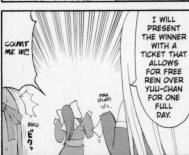

COUNT ME IN!!

I WILL PRESENT THE WINNER WITH A TICKET THAT ALLOWS FOR FREE REIN OVER YUU-CHAN FOR ONE FULL DAY.

PIRA (FLAP)

BIKU

TO EACH THEIR OWN

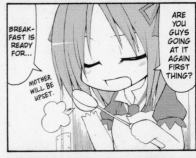

ARE YOU GUYS GOING AT IT AGAIN FIRST THING?

BREAK-FAST IS READY FOR...

MOTHER WILL BE UPSET.

THIS IS A WITCH WORTH FEARING. SHE KNOWS WHEN TO USE THE OLD CARROT ON A STICK.

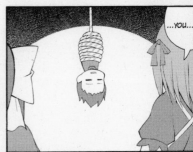

...YOU...

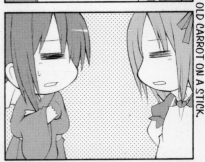

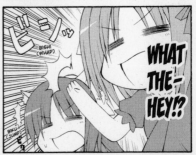

BISHI (WHAP)

WHAT THE- HEY!?

BIKU (JUMP)

28

THAT'S THE YOUNG LORD FOR YOU. THAT FELLOW JUST CAN'T READ THE SITUATION.

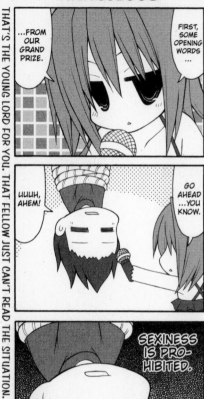

...FROM OUR GRAND PRIZE.

FIRST, SOME OPENING WORDS...

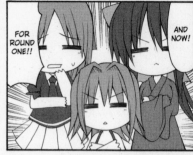

FOR ROUND ONE!!

AND NOW!

UUUH, AHEM!

GO AHEAD ...YOU KNOW.

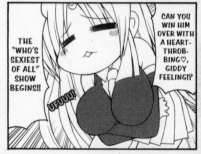

THE "WHO'S SEXIEST OF ALL" SHOW BEGINS!!

CAN YOU WIN HIM OVER WITH A HEART-THROB-BING♡ GIDDY FEELING!?

UFUUU!

SEXINESS IS PRO-HIBITED.

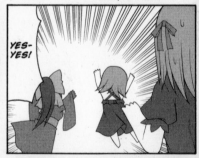

YES-YES!

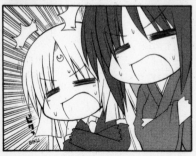

BIKU

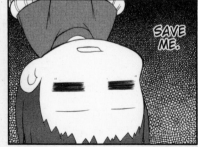

SAVE ME.

29

STRAY

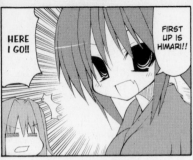

HERE I GO!!

FIRST UP IS HIMARI!!

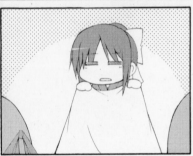

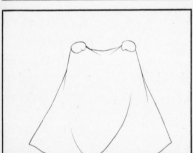

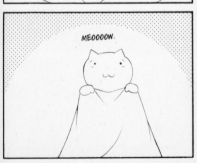

MEOOOOW.

IT SUITS YOU

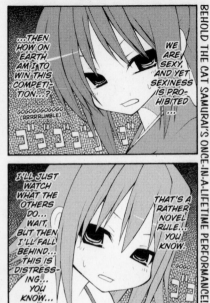

...THEN HOW ON EARTH AM I TO WIN THIS COMPETI-TION...?

WE ARE SEXY, AND YET SEXINESS IS PRO-HIBITED...

GOGOGOGOGOGO (RRRRRUMBLE)

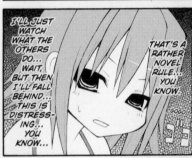

I'LL JUST WATCH WHAT THE OTHERS DO... WAIT, BUT THEN I'LL FALL BEHIND... THIS IS DISTRESS-ING... YOU KNOW...

THAT'S A RATHER NOVEL RULE!! YOU KNOW.

GOGO

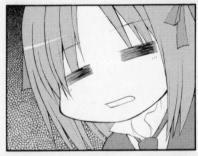

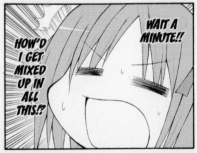

WAIT A MINUTE!!

HOW'D I GET MIXED UP IN ALL THIS!?

EEL

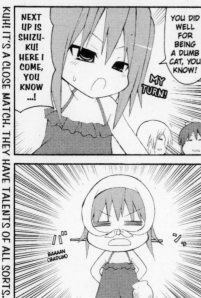

NEXT UP IS SHIZU-KU! HERE I COME, YOU KNOW ...!

YOU DID WELL FOR BEING A DUMB CAT, YOU KNOW!

MY TURN!

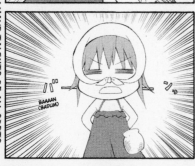

BAAAAN (BADUM)

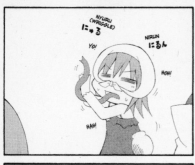

NYURU (WRIGGLE)
にゅる

NIRUN
にるん

YO!

HOH!

HAH!

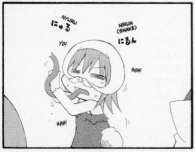

NYURU (WRIGGLE)
にゅる

NIRUN (SNAKE)
にるん

YO!

HOH!

HAH!

MAGIC

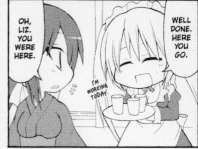

OH, LIZ. YOU WERE HERE.

I'M WORKING TODAY.

WELL DONE. HERE YOU GO.

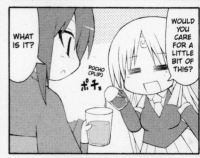

WHAT IS IT?

WOULD YOU CARE FOR A LITTLE BIT OF THIS?

POCHO (CLIP)
ポチ,

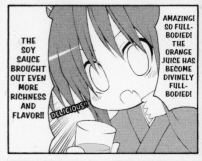

THE SOY SAUCE BROUGHT OUT EVEN MORE RICHNESS AND FLAVOR!!

DELICIOUS!!

AMAZING! SO FULL-BODIED! THE ORANGE JUICE HAS BECOME DIVINELY FULL-BODIED!

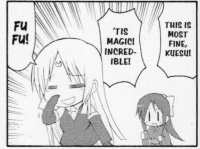

FU FU!

'TIS MAGIC! INCRED-IBLE!

THIS IS MOST FINE, KUESU!

31

OUT THE NOSE

MAGIC, TAKE 2

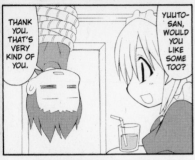

THANK YOU. THAT'S VERY KIND OF YOU.

YUUTO-SAN, WOULD YOU LIKE SOME TOO?

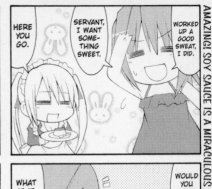

HERE YOU GO.

SERVANT, I WANT SOMETHING SWEET.

WORKED UP A GOOD SWEAT, I DID.

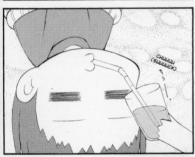

CHUUUU (SUUUUCK)

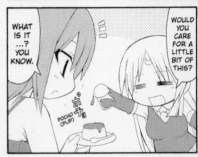

WHAT IS IT ...? YOU KNOW.

WOULD YOU CARE FOR A LITTLE BIT OF THIS?

POCHO (PLIP)

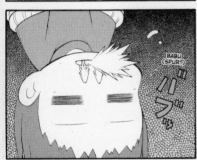

BABU (SPURT)

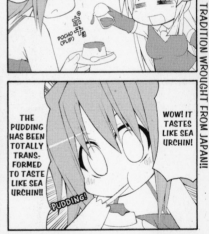

THE PUDDING HAS BEEN TOTALLY TRANSFORMED TO TASTE LIKE SEA URCHIN!!

WOW! IT TASTES LIKE SEA URCHIN!

PUDDING!

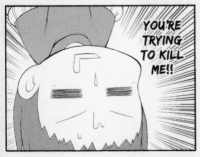

YOU'RE TRYING TO KILL ME!!

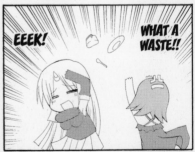

EEEK!

WHAT A WASTE!!

BOING

WESTERN HUMOR

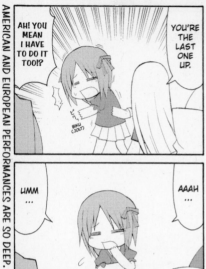

AH! YOU MEAN I HAVE TO DO IT TOO!?

YOU'RE THE LAST ONE UP.

ビクッ (BIKU)

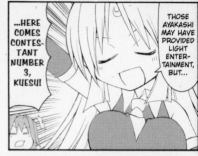

...HERE COMES CONTESTANT NUMBER 3, KUESU!

THOSE AYAKASHI MAY HAVE PROVIDED LIGHT ENTERTAINMENT, BUT...

UMM...

AAAH...

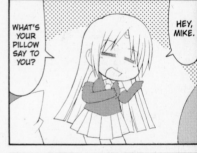

MY WIFE'S ALWAYS TELLING ME.

HEY, BOB.

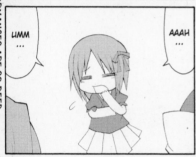

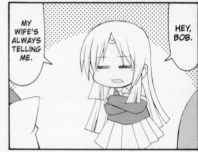

WHAT'S YOUR PILLOW SAY TO YOU?

HEY, MIKE.

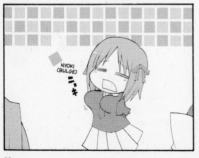

NYOKI (BULGE)

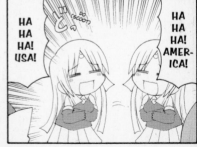

HA HA HA! USA!

ボ (SCOOT)

HA HA HA! AMERICA!

33

AND THE WINNER IS...?

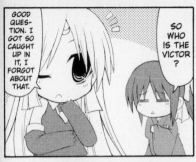

GOOD QUESTION. I GOT SO CAUGHT UP IN IT, I FORGOT ABOUT THAT.

SO WHO IS THE VICTOR?

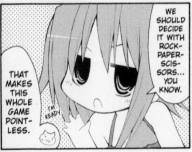

THAT MAKES THIS WHOLE GAME POINTLESS.

WE SHOULD DECIDE IT WITH ROCK-PAPER-SCISSORS... YOU KNOW.

I'M READY

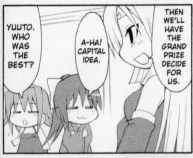

YUUTO. WHO WAS THE BEST?

A-HA! CAPITAL IDEA.

THEN WE'LL HAVE THE GRAND PRIZE DECIDE FOR US.

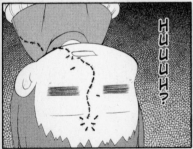

SURROUNDED ON ALL SIDES

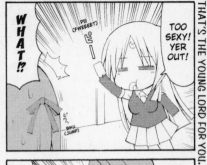

WHAT!?

(PII!) (FWEEEET)

TOO SEXY! YER OUT!

BIKU (JUMP)

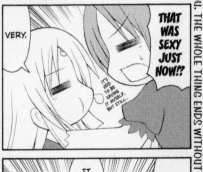

VERY.

IT'S ODD TO BE SAYING IT MYSELF, BUT STILL...

THAT WAS SEXY JUST NOW!?

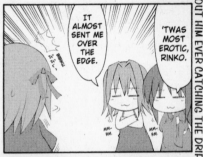

IT ALMOST SENT ME OVER THE EDGE.

'TWAS MOST EROTIC, RINKO.

MM-HM.

MM-HM.

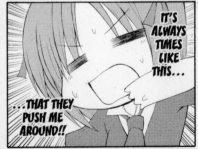

IT'S ALWAYS TIMES LIKE THIS...

...THAT THEY PUSH ME AROUND!!

THAT'S THE YOUNG LORD FOR YOU. THE WHOLE THING ENDS WITHOUT HIM EVER CATCHING THE DRIFT.

AND THERE YOU HAVE IT. MORE OF "HIMARI'S PANTIES" SERIALIZING IN DRAGON AGE NOW!

OMAHIMA CHRONICLE

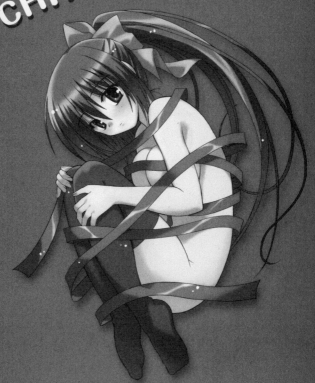

FROM HERE ON WE PRESENT TO YOU A
JAM-PACKED BREAKDOWN OF THE WORLD
OF *OMAMORI HIMARI* FOCUSING ON
ALL ITS CHARACTERS! SCENE BY SCENE,
WE'RE SENDING YOU 120% OF THE APPEAL
THAT THIS SERIES HAS TO OFFER!

"My duty is to protect you until your powers manifest."

A bodyguard with feelings that go beyond the need to fulfill a pledge.

WHEN YUUTO TURNS SIXTEEN, A FELINE AYAKASHI APPEARS BEFORE HIM IN ORDER TO FULFILL A PLEDGE FROM THE DAYS OF HER ANCESTORS. SHE PROCLAIMS HERSELF THE BODYGUARD WHO WILL PROTECT HIM FROM OTHER AYAKASHI WHO HAVE THEIR SIGHTS SET ON HIM. SHE HAS AN UNYIELDING PERSONALITY BUT HAS BEEN SMITTEN WITH YUUTO SINCE HIS CHILDHOOD AND IS CARRYING OUT HER DUTY ABOVE AND BEYOND THE MERE FULFILLMENT OF AN OATH. HER PERSONAL STYLE IS TRADITIONAL JAPANESE GARB, HER LONG BLACK HAIR TIED BACK IN A PONYTAIL USING A LARGE RED RIBBON. HER JEALOUS NATURE IS THE REASON SHE ABHORS THE PRESENCE OF SHIZUKU, LIZ, AND KUESU SO MUCH.

THE CAT AYAKASHI WHO GUARDS YUUTO

HIMARI

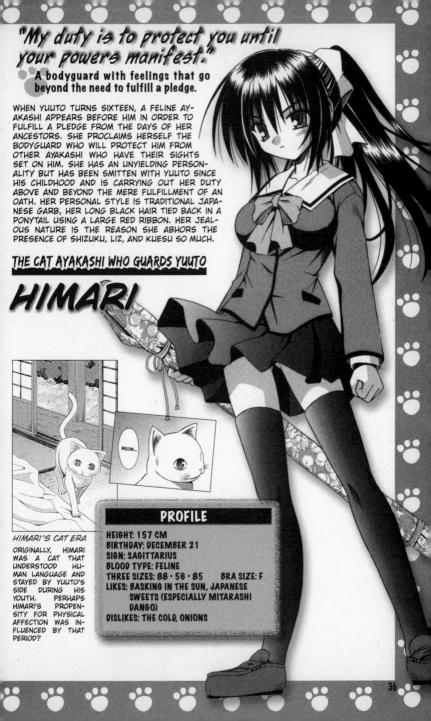

MEOW...

HIMARI'S CAT ERA

ORIGINALLY, HIMARI WAS A CAT THAT UNDERSTOOD HUMAN LANGUAGE AND STAYED BY YUUTO'S SIDE DURING HIS YOUTH. PERHAPS HIMARI'S PROPENSITY FOR PHYSICAL AFFECTION WAS INFLUENCED BY THAT PERIOD?

PROFILE

HEIGHT: 157 CM
BIRTHDAY: DECEMBER 21
SIGN: SAGITTARIUS
BLOOD TYPE: FELINE
THREE SIZES: 88 · 56 · 85   **BRA SIZE:** F
LIKES: BASKING IN THE SUN, JAPANESE SWEETS (ESPECIALLY MITARASHI DANGO)
DISLIKES: THE COLD, ONIONS

36

WHEN SHE GOES FROM HUMAN TO CAT-GIRL, HER POWERS ARE UNLEASHED. HER LIGHTNING FAST SPEED CAN BE ATTRIBUTED TO HER FELINE NATURE.

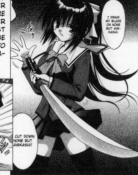

I DRAW MY BLADE ON NONE BUT AYAKASHI.

CUT DOWN NONE BUT AYAKASHI.

As a "bodyguard" constantly battling ayakashi

HIMARI USUALLY TAKES THE FORM OF A REGULAR HUMAN, BUT WHEN AYAKASHI APPEAR BEFORE HER, SHE ENTERS HER BATTLE MODE. WITH THE YASUTSUNA, A JAPANESE KATANA ENTRUSTED TO HER BY YUUTO'S GRANDFATHER GEN, SHE CUTS DOWN HER ENEMIES WITH THE DOWNRIGHT BRUTAL SKILL OF A MASTER SWORDSMAN. HOWEVER, AFTER YUUTO TOLD HER THAT HE FEARED WHAT THAT SAVAGENESS WAS DOING TO HER, SHE HAS BEEN SLOWLY BUT SURELY ADJUSTING HER STYLE OF COMBAT. IN BATTLE, HER ONLY VULNERABILITY IS WATER TOO DEEP FOR HER TO TREAD. RATHER CATLIKE, WOULDN'T YOU SAY?

...YOUNG LORD, SHALL WE RETURN HOME?

The mysterious, pretty transfer student who came to school

IN ORDER TO GUARD YUUTO AROUND THE CLOCK, HIMARI TOOK UP RESIDENCE IN THE AMAKAWA HOUSEHOLD. NATURALLY SHE ALSO ENROLLED AT TOURYOU HIGH TO AVOID BEING SEPARATED FROM YUUTO WHILE HE WAS AT SCHOOL. THERE, SHE TOOK THE NAME "HIMARI NOIHARA" AND BECAME THE CENTER OF ALL THE MALE STUDENTS' ATTENTION AS THE MYSTERIOUS, BUXOM TRANSFER STUDENT. MANY BOYS APPROACH HER, BUT SHE CONTINUALLY TURNS THEM DOWN WITH, "I ALREADY HAVE THE YOUNG LORD," LEAVING A TRAIL OF BROKEN HEARTS IN HER WAKE.

THIS IS THE TOURYOU SCHOOL UNIFORM IN ITS SUMMER VERSION. HERE SHE IS IN THE CLASSROOM AFTER SCHOOL WITH THE RAYS OF THE SETTING SUN ILLUMINATING HER.

WHEN SHE TURNS INTO HER CAT SELF, HIMARI LOSES HER INHIBITIONS AND TENDS TO MAKE BOLD MOVES. IS THIS HEAVEN FOR YUUTO? OR HELL?

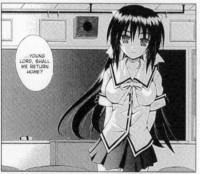

MEOW?

HIMARI.

I AM AN AYAKASHI TOO. I AM A CUTE CAT... ♡

Spend the night with her!? The sexy cat-girl

AS IN BATTLES WITH AYAKASHI, HIMARI'S CAT EARS AND TAIL TURN HER INTO A CAT-GIRL WHEN SHE BECOMES EXCITED. FOR THE SAKE OF PROTECTING (?) YUUTO, HIMARI STEALS INTO HIS BED NIGHT AFTER NIGHT, BUT SHE'S ALSO BEEN KNOWN TO GO FERAL ON HIM FROM TIME TO TIME. DESPITE HAVING SUCH A TEMPTING DISH SET RIGHT BEFORE HIM, YUUTO'S SEVERE ALLERGY TO CATS SETS HIM SNEEZING AND HIS EYES RUNNING, PUTTING THE WHOLE ORDEAL TO REST.

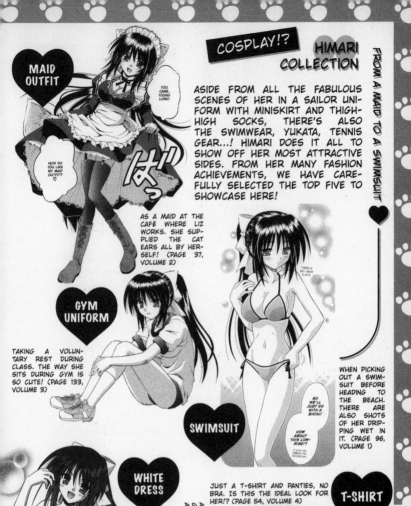

ASIDE FROM ALL THE FABULOUS SCENES OF HER IN A SAILOR UNIFORM WITH MINISKIRT AND THIGH-HIGH SOCKS, THERE'S ALSO THE SWIMWEAR, YUKATA, TENNIS GEAR...! HIMARI DOES IT ALL TO SHOW OFF HER MOST ATTRACTIVE SIDES. FROM HER MANY FASHION ACHIEVEMENTS, WE HAVE CAREFULLY SELECTED THE TOP FIVE TO SHOWCASE HERE!

MAID OUTFIT

YOU CAME, YOUNG LORD!

HOW DO YOU LIKE MY MAID OUTFIT?

AS A MAID AT THE CAFÉ WHERE LIZ WORKS. SHE SUPPLIED THE CAT EARS ALL BY HERSELF! (PAGE 37, VOLUME 2)

GYM UNIFORM

TAKING A VOLUNTARY REST DURING CLASS. THE WAY SHE SITS DURING GYM IS SO CUTE! (PAGE 133, VOLUME 3)

SWIMSUIT

THERE IS NOT MUCH CLOTH

SO WE'LL JUST GO WITH A BIKINI!

HOW ABOUT THIS LOW-RISE!?

WHEN PICKING OUT A SWIMSUIT BEFORE HEADING TO THE BEACH. THERE ARE ALSO SHOTS OF HER DRIPPING WET IN IT. (PAGE 96, VOLUME 1)

WHITE DRESS

A PRESENT FROM YUUTO. TRADITIONAL GARB SUITS HER, BUT SO DOES CASUAL ATTIRE! (PAGE 106, VOLUME 1)

TA-DA! WHAT DO YOU THINK?

JUST A T-SHIRT AND PANTIES, NO BRA. IS THIS THE IDEAL LOOK FOR HER!? (PAGE 54, VOLUME 4)

T-SHIRT

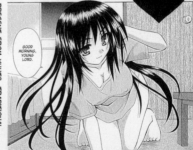

GOOD MORNING, YOUNG LORD.

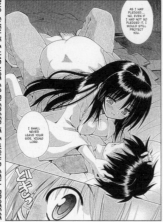

I SHALL NEVER LEAVE YOUR SIDE, YOUNG LORD.

AS I HAD PLEDGED... NO, EVEN IF I HAD NOT SO PLEDGED IT, I WOULD STILL PROTECT YOU.

"NO, EVEN IF I HAD NOT SO PLEDGED IT, I WOULD STILL PROTECT YOU," SHE SAYS, BUT THIS SITUATION LOOKS LIKE NOTHING SO MUCH AS SNEAKING INTO SOMEONE'S ROOM JUST TO GET IT ON!

When Himari met Yuuto

IMMEDIATELY AFTER HIMARI ENCOUNTERS YUUTO AND RINKO, SHE SUDDENLY PROCLAIMS, "HE IS MY MAN." SHE QUICKLY GETS THEM AWAY FROM AN AYAKASHI THAT HAS COME TO ATTACK YUUTO USING TAIZOU'S BODY. MEANWHILE, YUUTO IS GRILLED BY RINKO AS TO WHO THIS GIRL REALLY IS, THOUGH HE HIMSELF IS AT A COMPLETE LOSS TO ANSWER. EITHER WAY, HIMARI FORCES HERSELF INTO THE AMAKAWA HOUSEHOLD AND STARTS LIVING WITH YUUTO. WITH THIS SEXY COHABITANT SNEAKING INTO HIS BED, YUUTO QUICKLY FINDS HIMSELF WRAPPED AROUND HER LITTLE FINGER...

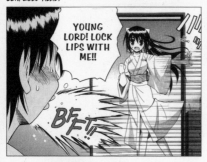

YOUNG LORD! LOCK LIPS WITH ME!!

BEFT!!

AFTER WITNESSING YUUTO AND KUESU KISS, HIMARI'S JEALOUSY PROPELS HER RIGHT TOWARD YUUTO TO CLEAR HER CONFUSED HEAD!

How far the two get

AFTER STARTING TO LIVE WITH EACH OTHER AND SPENDING SO MUCH TIME IN SCHOOL TOGETHER, YUUTO AND HIMARI GROW EVER CLOSER. AS HIMARI GETS TO KNOW THE YOUNG LORD AND HIS GENTLE AND KIND WAYS, SHE BEGINS TO DEVELOP FEELINGS FOR HIM THAT GO BEYOND THOSE OF A TYPICAL BODYGUARD ON DUTY. THEN, AFTER YUUTO'S SELF-PROCLAIMED BETROTHED KUESU ENTERS THE PICTURE, THE RELATIONSHIP BETWEEN THE TWO IS STEPPED UP A NOTCH. ONCE HIMARI WITNESSES YUUTO AND KUESU IN A KISS, SHE GOES AFTER YUUTO FOR A FIRST KISS OF HER OWN!

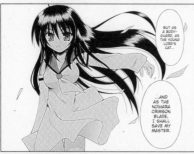

BUT AS A BODYGUARD, AS THE YOUNG LORD'S CAT...

...AND AS THE NOIHARA CRIMSON BLADE, I SHALL SAVE MY MASTER.

HIMARI SUDDENLY SHRINKS TO CHILD SIZE THANKS TO KUESU. SHE LOSES YASUTSUNA AND, UNABLE TO FIGHT, BEGINS TO AGONIZE OVER THE MEANING OF HER EXISTENCE. FORTUNATELY, SHE QUICKLY OVERCOMES HER SELF-DOUBT AND RETURNS TO BEING A BODYGUARD ONCE MORE.

Master & servant

YUUTO REMEMBERS WHEN HE MET HIMARI AS A YOUNG BOY. AFTER KUESU APPEARS, HIS FORGOTTEN PAST BECOMES EVEN CLEARER, AND THE TWO REALIZE THE DEPTH OF THEIR MASTER-SERVANT RELATIONSHIP. AT FIRST, HIMARI WAS ONLY CONCERNED WITH YUUTO ACCEPTING HIS DUTY AS A DEMON SLAYER, BUT SOON SHE ALSO BEGINS TO SHOW SIGNS OF UNDERSTANDING HIS DESIRE TO PEACEFULLY COEXIST WITH AYAKASHI. HOWEVER, AS NEW ENEMIES, BEGINNING WITH AGEHA, TAKE THE STAGE AND ATTACK YUUTO, IT SEEMS HER DUTY AS BODYGUARD WILL BE CONTINUING FOR A WHILE YET.

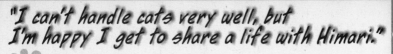

"I can't handle cats very well, but I'm happy I get to share a life with Himari."

🐾 **His once peaceful life is turned on its head on his sixteenth birthday.**

LOSING BOTH HIS PARENTS IN AN ACCIDENT SEVEN YEARS AGO, YUUTO IS LEFT ALL ALONE IN THE WORLD. WHEN HE WAS LITTLE, HE LIVED WITH HIS GRANDPARENTS ON THE AMAKAWA ESTATE IN NOIHARA IN ORDER TO INHERIT THE POSITION OF DEMON SLAYER, BUT WHEN HE ENTERED ELEMENTARY SCHOOL, HIS PARENTS MOVED HIM TO HIS CURRENT HOME.

LATER, A PROTECTIVE CHARM LEFT TO HIM BY HIS GRANDMOTHER SAWAKO SEALED AWAY HIS MEMORIES FROM NOIHARA, AND YUUTO SPENT HIS BOYHOOD WITH HIS HEART SHUT TIGHT. HOWEVER, HIS NEIGHBOR RINKO LOOKED AFTER HIM AND DID WHAT SHE COULD TO BRING BACK THE LIGHT TO HIS WORLD. AFTER HIS PARENTS DIED, YUUTO CONTINUED TO BE HELPED BY RINKO AND HER FAMILY AND LIVED A PEACEFUL LIFE.

THEN, ON THE DAY OF HIS SIXTEENTH BIRTHDAY, THE POWER OF THE CHARM WORE OFF AND EVERYTHING CHANGED. HE CAME TO BE TARGETED BY AYAKASHI FOR BEING A DEMON SLAYER AND GRADUALLY BEGAN TO REGAIN HIS MEMORIES. THEN HE BECAME PLAGUED BY THE EXPLOITS OF HIMARI, SHIZUKU, AND A WHOLE ONSLAUGHT OF NONHUMAN BEAUTIES...

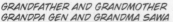

*GRANDFATHER AND GRANDMOTHER
GRANDPA GEN AND GRANDMA SAWA*

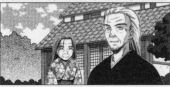

YUUTO'S GRANDPARENTS, DEMON SLAYERS. THEY LIVED ON THE AMAKAWA PROPERTY IN NOIHARA. WHEN YUUTO WAS YOUNG, HE USED TO LIVE WITH GRANDPA GEN, GRANDMA SAWA, AND HIMARI HERE.

SUCCESSOR OF THE DEMON-SLAYING AMAKAWA HOUSE

YUUTO AMAKAWA

PROFILE

HEIGHT: 165 CM **BIRTHDAY:** MAY 30
SIGN: GEMINI   **BLOOD TYPE:** B
LIKES: VIDEO GAMES, TELEVISION,
       MOVIES, THE INTERNET
DISLIKES: HIGH PLACES, FIGHTING

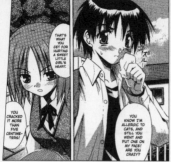

Yuuto is allergic to cats, and his bodyguard is a feline ayakashi!

EVERY MORNING, RINKO USED TO COME OVER TO WAKE YUUTO UP. THAT'S HOW MUCH SHE DOTED ON HIM. AND THE TWO WERE ENJOYING A PEACEFUL HIGH SCHOOL LIFE TOGETHER. YUUTO'S ONLY WORRY WAS RINKO'S PET CAT, RANMARU, WHOSE DANDER WOULD SET OFF HIS ALLERGIES. THEN HE FOUND HIMSELF BEING FORCED TO SHARE HIS HOME (AND BED) WITH HIMARI WHO INSISTS SHE'S HIS BODYGUARD. NOW WHENEVER SHE TURNS INTO HER CAT-GIRL SELF, THERE'S NO END TO THE TEARS AND SNEEZES. SO WHENEVER HIMARI SHOWS UP, RINKO TRIES SICCING RANMARU ON HER... NOW THAT HE'S THE OBJECT OF AFFECTION (AND TARGET OF JEALOUSY) FOR TWO GIRLS, WHERE WILL TOMORROW LEAD THIS UNFORTUNATE BOY!?

YUUTO'S THRILLED THAT SOMEONE WITH SUCH A HOT BODY AS HIMARI IS COMING ON TO HIM, BUT SHE MAKES RINKO GET PISSED OFF AT HIM...

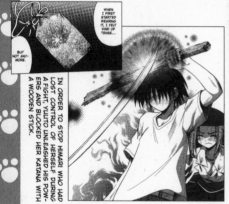

What it means to awaken as a demon slayer

BECAUSE THE SPELL YUUTO'S GRANDMA INFUSED INTO HIS PROTECTIVE CHARM WAS SO STRONG, HIS DEMON-SLAYER POWERS HAD STILL NOT AWAKENED BY THE TIME HE WAS SIXTEEN. HIS FEELINGS FOR HIMARI ULTIMATELY UNLEASH HIS POWERS. THEREAFTER, YUUTO HAS BEEN ABLE TO FIRE THE "LIGHT FERRY," A POWER THAT AMPLIFIES THE POTENTIAL OF A GIVEN OBJECT, FROM TIME TO TIME. HOWEVER, HE STILL SEEMS UNABLE TO USE IT AT WILL.

BOTH HIMARI AND KUESU SAY YUUTO'S TOO NICE, BUT IT'S LIKELY THAT PART OF HIM THAT MADE THEM FALL FOR HIM.

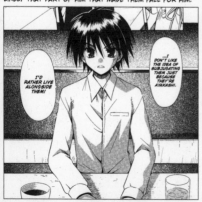

A pacifist who wants to keep the peace and live in harmony with ayakashi

EVEN IF HE POSSESSES THE POWER TO BE A DEMON SLAYER, YUUTO BELIEVES IT ISN'T RIGHT TO DESTROY AYAKASHI JUST BECAUSE OF WHAT THEY ARE. HE HOPES TO BE ABLE TO LIVE IN PEACE WITH AYAKASHI AND CONTINUE HIS THUS FAR PEACEFUL EXISTENCE. HOWEVER, WHEN HE WAS LITTLE, HE WAS ALL TOO EAGER TO BEAT UP THE BAD DEMONS. IT'S POSSIBLE THAT THE CHARM LEFT TO HIM WAS MEANT TO CHANGE THESE FEELINGS TOO.

"Looking at you guys, fighting you would be pointless."

● First she was the enemy, but suddenly she's a house-mate!?

SHIZUKU IS A MIZUCHI: A SNAKE AYAKASHI THAT MANIPULATES WATER. WHEN SHE FIRST SHOWED UP, SHE APPEARED SUDDENLY ON THE RIVERBANK AND LEFT YUUTO WITH THIS EERIE WARNING BEFORE RETURNING TO THE WATER: "FORGET EVERYTHING." IF SHE SUBMERGES HERSELF IN ENOUGH WATER, SHE CAN TURN HER OWN BODY INTO THE STUFF. AT FIRST, SHE WAS OUT TO DESTROY YUUTO, BUT SHE WAS TOUCHED BY HIS GENUINE KINDNESS AND HAD A CHANGE OF HEART. SHE EVEN ENDED UP LIVING WITH HIM. ON THE OUTSIDE, SHE'S A TEN-YEAR-OLD GIRL WITH A FLAT-AS-A-WALL BOSOM. IT SEEMS SHE'S CHOSEN TO GO THE ROUTE OF A LOLITA.

SHE WATCHES OVER YUUTO

SHIZUKU

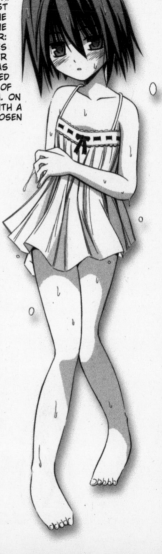

PROFILE

HEIGHT: 130 CM
BIRTHDAY: JANUARY 31 (SO SHE SAYS)
SIGN: AQUARIUS (SO SHE SAYS)
BLOOD TYPE: SNAKE
THREE SIZES: 60・45・72
BRA SIZE: AA
LIKES: BATHING, JAPANESE FOOD,
    CONFUSING HER OPPONENTS
DISLIKES: DIRTY WATER, RELIGIOUS
    RITUALS LIKE FESTIVALS

SHIZUKU AND HER SUPERNATURAL FRIENDS

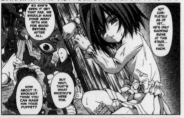

FEARING YUUTO AWAKENING TO HIS POWERS, THESE AYAKASHI SENT SHIZUKU AFTER HIM. SHE REPORTS ON HIS PROGRESS TO THEM OCCASIONALLY.

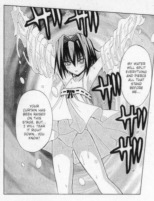

HERE IS SHIZUKU UNLEASHING A POWERFUL WATER ATTACK US-ING WATER. IF SHE USES PURE WATER, SHE CAN ALSO HEAL HUMAN WOUNDS.

MY WATER WILL SPLIT EVERYTHING AND PIERCE ALL THAT STAND BEFORE ME...

YOUR CURTAIN HAS BEEN RAISED ON THIS STAGE, BUT... I WILL TEAR IT RIGHT DOWN... YOU KNOW!

Her powers as a mizuchi that manipulates water

YOU WOULDN'T KNOW IT FROM HER PALE COMPLEXION, WHICH REMINDS YUUTO OF A "DROWNED CORPSE," BUT SHIZUKU CAN UN-LEASH CONSIDERABLE POWER IN BATTLE AS A MIZUCHI. SHE IS ABLE TO MANIPULATE WA-TER AND LAUNCH DAGGERS OF ICE CALLED "ICE NEEDLES" AND POWERFUL WATER MIS-SILES, AS WELL AS A VARIETY OF OTHER AT-TACKS. AND BECAUSE SHE CAN SUBSTITUTE OUT HER OWN BODY WITH BODIES OF WATER THAT HAVE A SIMILAR VOLUME, SHE CAN NIM-BLY EVADE PHYSICAL ATTACKS. SHIZUKU WAS ONCE WORSHIPPED AS A WATER GOD, WHICH GOES TO SHOW JUST HOW POWERFUL AN AYAKASHI SHE IS.

"THIS MORNING'S BREAKFAST IS TASTY AS EVER, SHIZUKU."

"OF COURSE, YOU KNOW... IT'S JUST FOR YOU, YUUTO... YOU KNOW."

AFTER LIVING TO-GETHER FOR QUITE SOME TIME, SHE BECOMES UNABLE TO HIDE HER AF-FECTION FOR YUU-TO. SHE'LL EVEN MURMUR TO HER-SELF LIKE THIS WHILE COOKING IN THE KITCHEN...

She takes the lead on chores in the Amakawa household and makes delicious meals

"HURRY UP AND EAT...YOU KNOW." HER WORDS MAY BE ROUGH, BUT HER COOKING SKILLS ARE LEAGUES ABOVE HIMARI'S OR RINKO'S. AFTER SHIZUKU COMES TO THE AMAKAWA HOUSE-HOLD, THE MEALS CONSIST OF TRADITIONAL JAPANESE CUISINE CENTERED AROUND WARM RICE DISHES. AND BEING A SNAKE THAT EN-JOYS CLEAN, CLEAR WATER, SHE ALSO LIKES TO KEEP THINGS CLEAN AND IS VERY SKILLED AT BOTH TIDYING UP AND LAUNDRY. WHEN HI-MARI REALIZES THAT SHE'LL NEVER BEAT SHI-ZUKU WHEN IT COMES TO DOMESTIC AFFAIRS, SHE TAKES UP THAT PART-TIME JOB AT THE MAID CAFÉ.

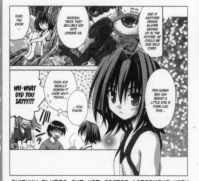

OKAY, YOU KNOW...

SHIZUKU'S TRICK THAT BROUGHT KID INTO JOINING US.

AND IF ANOTHER DEMON SLAYER SHOWS UP IN THE FUTURE, HE COULD BE OUR WILD CARD.

WH-WHAT DID YOU SAYYY!!!

THIS KID REALLY DOESN'T HIDE ANY-THING...

...YOU KNOW.

FEW HUMAN MEN CAN RESIST A LITTLE GIRL'S FORM LIKE THIS...

SHIZUKU BLURTS OUT HER SECRET AGREEMENT WITH THE OTHER AYAKASHI. IS SHE JUST BEING TRANSPAR-ENT, OR IS SHE PLOTTING SOMETHING...?

She's a straightforward Lolita with an ulterior motive in mind...even now!?

THOUGH SHE WAS SUPPOSED TO TAKE YUUTO'S LIFE, SHIZUKU ENDS UP HEAD OF HOUSEKEEPING IN THE AMAKAWA HOME IN A MATTER OF DAYS. SHE REVEALS THAT THIS UNBELIEVABLE CHANGE OF HEART WAS RE-QUIRED OF HER IN ORDER TO TRICK YUUTO. AS SHE EXPLAINS TO RINKO, "FEW HUMAN MEN CAN RESIST A LITTLE GIRL'S FORM LIKE THIS...YOU KNOW." WHEN HIMARI IS TURNED INTO A LITTLE GIRL TOO, SHIZUKU BECOMES QUITE UNHAPPY, SAYING, "THERE'S ONLY ROOM ENOUGH HERE FOR ONE LOLITA CHAR-ACTER...YOU KNOW."

COSPLAY!?

SHIZUKU COLLECTION

FROM SCHOOL SWIMSUITS TO DRESSES!

SHIZUKU LIKES TO DRESS IN WAYS THAT INTENTIONALLY ACCENTUATE HER LOLITA-NESS AND GIVE THE READERS A GOOD SHOW. STARTING WITH HER IRON-GRAY SCHOOL SWIMSUIT, YOU EVEN GET TO SEE SHOTS OF HER WITH WETNESS RUNNING DOWN HER THIGHS. AND AS A SNAKE WHO LOVES WATER, THE WAY SHE ALWAYS KEEPS HERSELF SOMEWHAT WET AND DAMP IS ANOTHER OF HER SELLING POINTS. SHIZUKU NOT ONLY LEADS YUUTO BUT ALSO HIS FELLOW CLASSMATES AROUND BY THE NOSE, AS SHE ALWAYS KEEPS UP A COOL ATTITUDE WHILE INDULGING IN HER PENCHANT FOR PROVIDING FAN SERVICE SHOTS.

SCHOOL SWIMSUIT

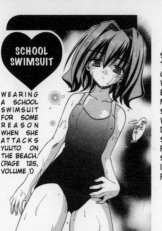

WEARING A SCHOOL SWIMSUIT FOR SOME REASON WHEN SHE ATTACKS YUUTO ON THE BEACH. (PAGE 125, VOLUME 1)

BLACK DRESS

A SIMPLE BLACK DRESS WITH PRETTY FLOWERS DECORATING THE BOSOM. (PAGE 86, VOLUME 2)

......?

MAID OUTFIT

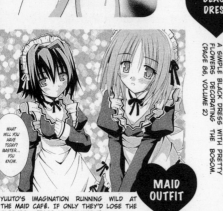

WHAT WILL YOU HAVE TODAY? MASTER... YOU KNOW.

YUUTO'S IMAGINATION RUNNING WILD AT THE MAID CAFÉ. IF ONLY THEY'D LOSE THE SLEEVES... (PAGE 42, VOLUME 2)

SWIMSUIT... OR SHOULD WE SAY THREADS!?

I'M LOOKING TO STAND OUT ONSTAGE WITH THIS BOLD SWIMWEAR... YOU KNOW.

...WHOA, SHIZUKU!?

THE BATHING SUIT SHE COMPETED IN AT THE SCHOOL FESTIVAL SWIMSUIT COMPETITION!? (PAGE 54, VOLUME 5)

DRIPPING-WET DRESS

...WHO COULD BE ATTRACTED TO THE SCENT OF A DEMON SLAYER... YOU KNOW.

THERE ARE STILL WILD AYAKASHI IN THIS AREA...

OH WELL... IF THE CAT'S WITH HIM, HE'LL MANAGE SOMEHOW... YOU KNOW.

BEWITCHING YUUTO'S CLASSMATES, SHE PROBABLY GOT THE ATTENTION OF MANY READERS IN THIS POSE TOO. (PAGE 96, VOLUME 4)

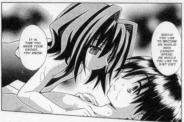

BECOME AN INVALID OR DIE. WEARING A SCHOOL SWIM-SUIT, SHIZUKU GIVES YUUTO THESE TWO CRUEL CHOIC-ES. AT THIS POINT IN TIME, SHIZUKU WAS AN ENEMY AFTER YUUTO'S LIFE.

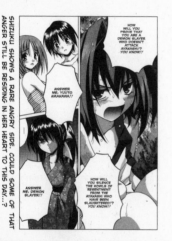

"BESIDES, IF I'M GOING TO SLEEP...I'LL DO IT IN YUU-TO'S BED...YOU KNOW.♥" SUCH A SWEET DECLARATION IS LIKE SOMETHING HIMARI WOULD SAY!

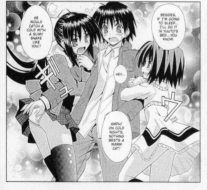

When Shizuku met Yuuto

APPROXIMATELY A CENTURY AGO, SHIZUKU'S TRIBE LIVED IN A LAKE AND WERE WOR-SHIPPED AS WATER GODS. HOWEVER, THEY WERE SUDDENLY MASSACRED BY A SINGLE DEMON-SLAYER FAMILY, THE JIBASHIRI. THAT'S WHY SHE CARRIES A GRUDGE AGAINST SELF-ISH HUMANS AND DEMON SLAYERS AND TRIED TO KILL YUUTO WHEN HE TURNED SIXTEEN AND WAS IN DANGER OF AWAKENING TO HIS SLAYER POWERS. HOWEVER, IN HER FIRST FIGHT WITH YUUTO, SHE WITNESSED HOW HE TREATED HIMARI AND WASN'T AS CONFIDENT IN HER DECISION TO EXTRACT REVENGE, DE-CIDING INSTEAD TO TAKE UP RESIDENCE WITH HIM UNDER THE PRETEXT OF KEEPING HIM UN-DER SURVEILLANCE.

The two in the present

"HOW WILL YOU PROVE THAT YOU ARE A DEMON SLAYER WHO DOESN'T ATTACK AY-AKASHI!? YOU KNOW!!" "HOW WILL YOU SI-LENCE THE HOWLS OF RESENTMENT FROM THE AYAKASHI WHO HAVE BEEN SLAUGH-TERED!? YOU KNOW!!" WHEN SHIZUKU INTER-ROGATES YUUTO WITH THESE QUESTIONS, HE ANSWERS WITH SINCERITY AND KINDNESS. AFTER THAT, SHIZUKU CLAIMS TO JUST BE KEEPING AN EYE ON HIM, BUT HER FEELINGS TOWARD YUUTO BEGIN TO CHANGE INTO AF-FECTION. SHE EVEN RESEARCHES DEMON SLAYERS FOR HIM AND AIDS HIM IN HIS TRAIN-ING... EVEN NOW, YUUTO REGARDS SHIZUKU WITH SOME DEGREE OF FEAR BUT STILL HAS FAITH IN HER AS A FRIEND.

Both near and far today

WHEN SHIZUKU LEARNS OF THE KISS SHARED BETWEEN KUESU AND YUUTO, SHE'S BADLY AGITATED. DESPITE AN UP-ROAR FROM RINKO, SHE ALSO TRIES TO GET A TASTE OF WHAT THAT'S LIKE AND PRESSES YUUTO WITH HER EXTRA-LONG TONGUE TO LOCK LIPS WITH HIM. AFTER THAT, SHE WARNS THAT "EITHER WAY, I WILL HAVE...ALL OF YOU...YOU KNOW." WHILE KEEPING A CERTAIN AMOUNT OF DISTANCE BETWEEN HERSELF AND YUUTO, SHE STILL BEGINS TO SHOW FEELINGS FOR HIM. WHETHER SHIZUKU'S WARNING WAS OUT OF HER ATTACHMENT TO HIM OR UNDER ORDERS IS YET TO BE REVEALED.

"So long as Yuuto ties this ribbon in my hair, I'll be a cute little girl."

The admirable young girl who supports Yuuto.

EVERY MORNING, RINKO BARGES INTO YUUTO'S HOME AND EVEN COMES INTO HIS ROOM TO GIVE HIM A RUDE AWAKENING WITH HER PET CAT RANMARU. THAT'S HOW CLOSE OF A CHILDHOOD FRIEND SHE IS. SHE'S ALSO IN THE SAME CLASS AS HIM, AND EVER SINCE SHE BECAME HIS NEIGHBOR AS A LITTLE KID, SHE'S BEEN LOOKING OUT FOR HIM. BEHIND THE FACADE OF FRIENDSHIP, RINKO'S HEART ACTUALLY BURNS WITH LOVE FOR HER DEAR FRIEND. SHE EXCELS IN SPORTS AND IS CALLED THE BEST SUBSTITUTE PLAYER FOR ALL THE SPORTS CLUBS AT SCHOOL. SHE'S SMALL BREASTED AND HATES WHEN THAT'S POINTED OUT TO HER.

YUUTO'S CHILDHOOD FRIEND
RINKO KUZAKI

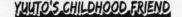

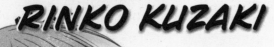

PROFILE
HEIGHT: 156.5 CM
BIRTHDAY: APRIL 9
SIGN: ARIES   BLOOD TYPE: A
THREE SIZES: 75 • 57 • 84
BRA SIZE: A
LIKES: EXERCISE, CATS, FASHION
      MAGAZINES, COMEDY SHOWS
DISLIKES: THINGS THAT AREN'T CLEAR,
         ENGLISH, MATH

YUUTO'S SECOND MOTHER!?
RINKO'S MOM

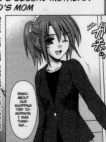

RINKO AND HER MOTHER HAVE LOOKED AFTER YUTO TO EVER SINCE HE LOST HIS PARENTS. SHE CALLS HER DAUGHTER "RINKO" AND YUUTO "YUUTO-KUN."

RINKO, ABOUT OUR SHOPPING TRIP TO-MORROW, I WAS THINK-ING...

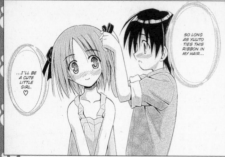

HIS FIRST GIFT OF RIBBONS WAS WHEN THEY WERE IN ELEMENTARY SCHOOL. EVER SINCE THEN, THEY'VE KEPT UP THE YEARLY TRADITION AS A SIGN OF THEIR DEEP BOND.

Her trademark red ribbons and the burning memories they carry

RINKO ALWAYS WEARS HER HAIR UP IN TWO RED RIBBONS AND ONLY TAKES THEM OFF WHEN SHE GOES TO SLEEP OR TAKES A BATH. THIS IS BECAUSE EVERY YEAR ON THE NIGHT OF THE SUMMER FESTIVAL, YUUTO BUYS HER THESE PROMISED RIBBONS. HER OLD RIBBONS GET TIED AROUND A TREE BEHIND A SHINTO SHRINE, AND YUUTO TIES THE NEW ONES ON HER HAIR AS PART OF A TRADITION JUST BETWEEN THEM. THE RIBBONS ARE PROOF OF A PRECIOUS MEMORY THAT BINDS RINKO AND YUUTO TOGETHER.

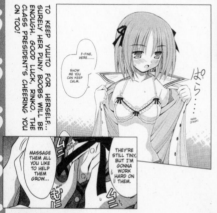

Rinko panics in the face of new rivals—"But in the end, he's a human."

HIMARI, KUESU, AND LIZ—AS ONE GIRL AFTER ANOTHER POPS UP IN YUUTO'S LIFE, RINKO STARTS PANICKING, RECALLING HOW "BEFORE, IT WAS NORMAL TO JUST BE THE TWO OF US" AND "AMAKAWA ALREADY HAS KUZAKI." WHILE FRETTING OVER HOW TO KEEP YUUTO ALL TO HERSELF, SHE REASONS THAT THE REST OF THEM ARE ALL JUST AYAKASHI. EXCEPT KUESU... AND SO HER WORRIES ONLY DEEPEN. IS HER ONLY OPTION TO ATTACK USING SEX APPEAL!?

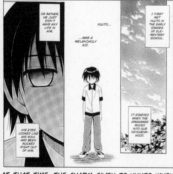

AT THAT TIME, THE CHARM GIVEN TO YUUTO WHEN HIS PARENTS TOOK HIM AWAY FROM HIS GRANDPA AND GRANDMA WAS WHAT SEALED HIS HEART OFF TO EMOTION.

Being his childhood friend, she knows Yuuto's dark past.

RINKO MET YUUTO WHEN THEY STARTED ELEMENTARY SCHOOL. IT ALL BEGAN WHEN THE AMAKAWAS MOVED INTO THE NEIGHBORHOOD. AT THAT TIME, YUUTO WAS GLOOMY, IF NOT DOWNRIGHT LIFELESS. RINKO COULDN'T SIMPLY LEAVE YUUTO LIKE THAT, SO SHE STARTED WALKING TO SCHOOL WITH HIM AND PLAYING WITH HIM UNTIL HE SLOWLY BUT SURELY CHANGED. ON THE DAY THAT HIS PARENTS DIED, THE TWO OF THEM WEPT TOGETHER. THE REASON WHY YUUTO IS AS OPTIMISTIC AS HE IS TODAY IS BECAUSE OF RINKO'S EFFORTS WHEN THEY WERE LITTLE KIDS.

"Y-Yuuto-san! I am your maid, and you are my master! I will serve you in all ways, twenty-four hours a day..."

🐾 Please, be my master! ❤

THE WELL-ENDOWED MAID WHO WORKS AT CAFÉ RELISH. HER TRUE FORM IS A TSUKUMOGAMI THAT INHABITS A TEACUP. FOR THE SAKE OF EXPOSING THE WORLD TO DELICIOUS TEA, SHE CAME FROM ENGLAND TO JAPAN ONE HUNDRED YEARS AGO AND PROCLAIMED HERSELF A "TEA SPIRIT." WHEN SHE FIRST APPEARED, SHE CLAIMED, "GIVING SUCH A SURPLUS OF ATTENTION TO ONE ALONE GOES AGAINST THE WAY OF WAITRESSING!!" BUT AFTER YUUTO SAVED HER LIFE, SHE HAS SINCE GONE BACK ON HER WORD. SHE JUSTIFIES IT BY SAYING THAT "YUUTO-SAN ISN'T 'ONE SPECIFIC CUSTOMER.' HE'S MY SIGNIFICANT OTHER." WHEN IT COMES TO YUUTO, SHE GETS FLUSTERED IN HER SPEECH AND ACTIONS. IS IT GENUINE OR JUST A FARCE!?

A TEA SPIRIT!?
LIZLET L. CHELSIE

THE CAFÉ OWNER WHO ALSO OWNS LIZ'S TEACUP HAS A FAMILY SO HE RETURNS HOME AFTER WORK, WHILE LIZ LIVES IN A PERSONAL ROOM PREPARED FOR HER ON THE SECOND STORY OF THE SHOP.

THE BRAVE MASTER OF CAFÉ RELISH WHO HIRED LIZ

PROFILE

HEIGHT: 157 CM
BIRTHDAY: FEBRUARY 22 (NOT THE DAY SHE WAS MANUFACTURED, BUT THE DAY SHE FIRST TOOK PHYSICAL FORM)
SIGN: PISCES   **BLOOD TYPE:** TEA
THREE SIZES: 91 · 57 · 87   **BRA SIZE:** G
LIKES: TEA, SCONES, MAID OUTFITS
DISLIKES: PAINFUL THINGS, VIOLENCE

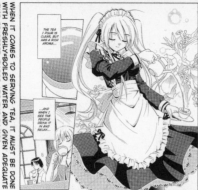

When it comes to serving tea, it must be done with freshly-boiled water and given adequate time to steep. Those are the basics.

To spread the deliciousness of tea, she came to Japan from England a mere hundred years ago

"THE TEA I POUR IS CLEAR, BUT HAS A RICH AROMA...AND WHEN I SEE THE PEOPLE DRINK IT IN AND RELAX..." THOSE ARE THE FEELINGS LIZ HAS ABOUT WORKING AT THE CAFÉ. SHE GROWS FRESH HERBS FOR HER HERBAL TEAS. THAT'S JUST HOW SERIOUS SHE IS ABOUT TEA. HER STATUS AS A SELF-PROCLAIMED TEA SPIRIT IS APPARENTLY SINCERE.

She mistakes Himari and Yuuto as ganging up to kill her. That's when she sneaks the poison into his tea.

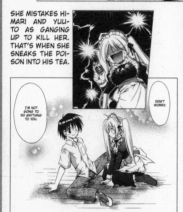

She meant to poison him, but... she instantly fell for Yuuto

WHEN YUUTO FIRST VISITED THE CAFÉ, LIZ THOUGHT THAT HE WAS A GHOST HUNTER OUT TO EXTERMINATE HER. TO PROTECT HER PEACEFUL, TEA-CENTRIC LIFE, SHE TRIED TO POISON YUUTO'S DRINK. BUT SHIZUKU SAW THROUGH HER PLAN, AND LIZ FOUND HERSELF BATTLING AN ENRAGED HIMARI RIGHT IN THE SHOP. IN THE MIDST OF THE BATTLE, THE TEACUP LIZ INHABITED WAS IN DANGER OF BEING SHATTERED, BUT IT WAS CAUGHT IN MIDAIR BY YUUTO. THE FACT THAT HE SAVED HER LIFE DRIVES THE HEART IN HER AMPLE BOSOM TO BEAT ESPECIALLY FAST!

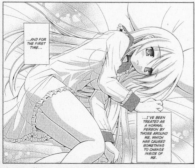

AFTER COMING IN CONTACT WITH SO MANY PEOPLE AND EXPERIENCING HER FIRST CRUSH, LIZ HAS STARTED SPENDING MORE TIME AS A HUMAN.

She's not human, but... this burning feeling is a first for her

LIZ LIVES ON THE SECOND FLOOR OF CAFÉ RELISH. BACK WHEN SHE LIVED IN EDINBURGH, SHE WENT THE WAY OF THE TSUKUMOGAMI (?) AND WOULD REVERT BACK TO HER ORIGINAL FORM AS A TEACUP. BUT NOW SHE GOES TO BED IN HER HUMAN FORM. THIS IS ALL DUE TO THE FACT THAT SHE'S FALLEN FOR YUUTO. SHE DREAMS OF CATERING TO YUUTO AND FANTASIZES ABOUT ONE DAY SERVING HIM HER SPECIALLY BREWED MILK TEA.

"I am Kuesu, heiress to the Jinguuji clan of the twelve demon-slayer families."

A powerful demon slayer who uses magic.

UNLIKE YUUTO WHO FORGOT HIS CHILDHOOD, KUESU HAS ALWAYS BEEN AWARE OF HER DEMON-SLAYER DUTIES. "WE ARE THE CHOSEN ONES. HAVING BEEN GRANTED SUPERNATURAL POWERS, WE MUST ERADICATE THOSE FILTHY AYAKASHI FOR THE SAKE OF THE PLANET AND ITS PEOPLE." SHE HAS STUDIED WESTERN MAGIC FOR MANY YEARS AND SEEKS TO STAND AT THE PINNACLE OF ALL THE DEMON-SLAYER FAMILIES, SO SHE REGARDS ALL AYAKASHI AS THE ENEMY. HOWEVER, BECAUSE SHE IS FRIENDS WITH YUUTO WHO HAS BEFRIENDED HIMARI AND SHIZUKU, KUESU HAS AGREED TO TEMPORARILY CALL A TRUCE.

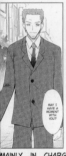

KUESU'S PERSONAL AID: KABURAGI FROM UNIT 4 OF THE DEFENSE BRANCH FOR PUBLIC PEACE

MAY I HAVE A MOMENT WITH YOU?

MAINLY IN CHARGE OF COVERING UP KUESU'S MESSES AFTER SHE'S GONE BERSERK. HE AIDS HER IN HER MISSIONS.

YUUTO'S FIANCÉE!?

KUESU JINGUUJI

PROFILE

HEIGHT: 158 CM
BIRTHDAY: OCTOBER 17
SIGN: LIBRA   BLOOD TYPE: AB
THREE SIZES: 86 · 56 · 85   BRA SIZE: E
LIKES: READING, RESEARCHING MAGIC,
          NEW KNOWLEDGE
DISLIKES: CATS, ALL AYAKASHI, IGNORANCE

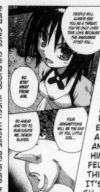

PEOPLE WILL ALWAYS SEE YOU AS A THREAT. YOU'VE ONLY LIVED THIS LONG BECAUSE THE AYAKASHI PITIED YOU...

SO STAY AWAY FROM HIM.

GO AHEAD AND TRY TO SUBJUGATE ME, DEMON SLAYER.

YOUR ASSUMPTIONS WILL BE THE END OF YOU, LITTLE GIRL.

EVER SINCE CHILDHOOD, KUESU HASN'T BELIEVED IN THE ABILITY OF HUMANS AND AYAKASHI TO TRUST ONE ANOTHER. THAT'S PROBABLY WHY SHE IS SO OPPOSED TO HIMARI.

Kuesu and Himari's connection from long ago

WHILE YUUTO AND HIMARI ARE ENJOYING THEIR WALK HOME FROM SCHOOL ONE DAY, THEY ARE SUDDENLY AT- TACKED BY KUESU AND HER MAGIC. YUUTO'S FORGOTTEN ALL ABOUT KUESU, BUT HE'S ENGAGED TO HER, AND HE SPENT SOME TIME WITH HER IN HIS GRANDPARENTS' HOUSE WHEN THEY WERE BOTH LITTLE. FROM THAT VERY EARLY TIME, KUESU HAS BEEN DEDICATED TO HER DUTIES AS A DEMON SLAYER AND HAS NEVER BELIEVED THAT HUMANS AND AYAKASHI COULD GET ALONG, HENCE HER DISLIKE FOR HIMARI, WHO IN THE PAST ALWAYS STUCK BY YUUTO IN HER FELINE AYAKASHI FORM. HIMARI, ON THE OTHER HAND, DID NOT THINK VERY FONDLY OF THIS GIRL COMING ON TO HER YUUTO. IT'S TRUE THAT YUUTO DOESN'T KNOW ANYTHING ABOUT KUE- SU, BUT THE BOND BETWEEN THE TWO RUNS DEEP.

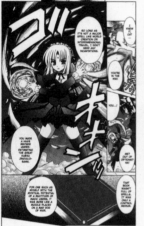

I KNEW IT!

SO LONG AS IT'S NOT A MAJOR SPELL LIKE WORLD CREATION OR INTERDIMENSIONAL TRAVEL, I DON'T NEED ANY INCANTATIONS.

YOU'RE IN THE WAY.

YOU...!

YOU MADE A HUGE MISTAKE UNDER- ESTIMATING THE GREAT KUESU JINGUUJI- SAMA.

GET OUT OF MY WAY.

THAT BOOK WASN'T FULL OF SPELLS. IT WAS ONLY A MUZZLE PLACED ON A MAD DOG OF WAR.

FOR ONE SUCH AS MYSELF WITH THE MYSTICAL POTENTIAL OF A MULTITUDE OF MAGIC USERS, IT WAS MORE LIKE A MUZZLE PLACED ON A MAD DOG OF WAR.

A MASTER OF VERY POWERFUL SPELLS, KUESU BELIEVES MAGICAL TOMES ARE NOTHING MORE THAN MEANS OF CONTROLLING AND LIMITING HER POWER. SHE SAYS THAT UNLESS IT'S A VERY MASSIVE ATTACK, SHE DOESN'T EVEN REALLY NEED TO CHANT MAGICAL INCANTATIONS.

The Jinguuji family of demon slayers relies on Western magic

COMPARED TO THE OTHER DEMON-SLAYER FAMILIES, THE JINGUUJI HAVE A SHORT HIS- TORY. IN THE AGE WHERE SWORDS AND YIN AND YANG SPIRITUALISM WERE MOST WIDELY USED, THEY RELIED ON MAGIC. THIS RESULT- ED IN THEIR BEING LABELED "PAGANS." TO DO AWAY WITH THAT HUMILIATION, THE JIN- GUUJI DEVOTED THEMSELVES TO WESTERN MAGIC AND NOW AIM TO STAND AT THE TOP OF THE TWELVE FAMILIES. KUESU HERSELF STUDIED ABROAD AT THE ROYAL MAGIC SOCI- ETY IN ENGLAND AND STUDIED THE CLASS-1 FORBIDDEN TEXTS OF LEMEGETON. NOW HER POWERS ARE VERY MUCH SOMETHING TO CONTEND WITH.

When she's ticked off, she loves to say, "<DEATH> be with you!"

KUESU USUALLY SPEAKS QUITE PROP- ERLY, BUT WHEN HER BLOOD STARTS TO BOIL IN A FIGHT, HER SUPER-SADISTIC SIDE COMES THROUGH. WHILE LAUNCH- ING EXTREMELY POWERFUL ATTACKS, SHE'LL YELL, "<DEATH> BE WITH YOU!" A VARIATION TO THAT IS "YOU WANNA DIE!?" IN ANY CASE, SHE HAS ABSOLUTE CON- FIDENCE IN HER ABILITIES AND READILY LOOKS DOWN ON OTHERS.

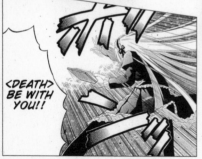

<DEATH> BE WITH YOU!!

INSULTED BY SHIZUKU, SHE SNAPS AND YELLS, "YOU STEAMING PILE OF SHIT!!" WHILE LAUNCHING THIS AT- TACK. IF YOU CARELESSLY PROVOKE HER, <DEATH> WILL BE WITH YOU, YA HEAR!?

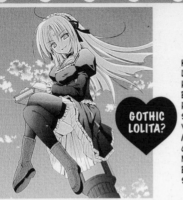

COSPLAY!?

KUESU COLLECTION

KUESU-SAMA WEARS HER HAIR LONG AND STRAIGHT WITH A FRILLY HEADBAND. HER TRADEMARK SYMBOL IS THE CRESCENT MOON ON HER FOREHEAD. WITH HER ALMOND-SHAPED EYES, SHE ALWAYS GETS VIOLENT ON THE ONE SHE LOVES MOST, AND HER FAVORITE FASHION IS GOTHIC LOLITA WITH ALL ITS BLACKNESS. HERE WE'VE COLLECTED THE BEST SCENES THAT HIGHLIGHT HER STUCK-UP PRINCESS (?) AIR!

GOTHIC LOLITA?

KUESU'S DEBUT SCENE, WEARING THE SLEEK STYLE THAT COULD BE CALLED HER DEFAULT OUTFIT. (PAGE 70, VOLUME 3)

KUESU-SAMA WITH A WICKED GRIN ON HER FACE. TO THINK A WITCH HAT WOULD LOOK SO GOOD ON HER! (PAGE 140, VOLUME 3)

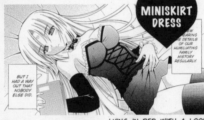

MINISKIRT DRESS

...HEARING THE DETAILS OF OUR HUMILIATING FAMILY HISTORY REGULARLY.

BUT I HAD A WAY OUT THAT NOBODY ELSE DID.

LYING IN BED WITH A LOOK OF ENNUI ON HER FACE. AND A PANTY SHOT FOR GOOD MEASURE... (PAGE 113, VOLUME 3)

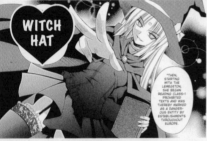

WITCH HAT

*THEN, STARTING WITH THE LEMEGETON, SHE BEGAN READING CLASS-I PROHIBITED TEXTS AND WAS THEREBY MARKED AS A DANGEROUS ENTITY BY ESTABLISHMENTS THROUGHOUT EUROPE.

SCHEMING ON HER BED. THE HIGHLIGHT TO THIS GETUP IS THE THREE RIBBONS. (PAGE 13, VOLUME 5)

MINISKIRT DRESS 2

YOU WOULDN'T HAPPEN TO HAVE TURNED INTO A CUTE LITTLE KITTEN, NOW WOULD YOU?

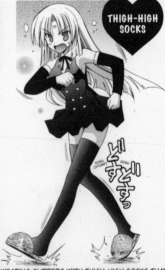

THIGH-HIGH SOCKS

DOSU (STOMP) DOSU DOSU

WEARING SLIPPERS WITH THIGH-HIGH SOCKS THAT HUG HER SLENDER LEGS. (PAGE 37, VOLUME 4)

FROM A WITCH HAT TO A MINISKIRT

52

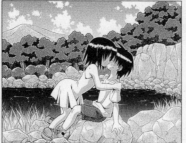

KUESU AND YUUTO'S FIRST KISS BY THE LAKE. BUT WHEN YUUTO INITIALLY RECALLS IT AFTER HIS LOST MEMORIES RETURN, HE MISTAKES THE GIRL IN HIS MEMORY FOR HIMARI.

When Kuesu met Yuuto

WHEN YUUTO WAS A CHILD, HE WAS INTRODUCED TO KUESU, AND THE TWO WERE BETROTHED IN AN EFFORT TO MERGE THE AMAKAWA AND JINGUUJI FAMILIES. THE TWO CHILDREN IMMEDIATELY HIT IT OFF, AND YUUTO EVEN SAID, "YOU'RE A DEMON SLAYER TOO, KUESU-CHAN? THEN LET'S BOTH WORK TOGETHER TO DO OUR BEST." TO WHICH SHE REPLIED, "I CAN HANDLE THIS ALONE BY MYSELF." THOUGH SHE ALWAYS HAD A HABIT OF LASHING OUT AT THE PEOPLE SHE CARED ABOUT, THE TWO HAD A SOLID AND HAPPY FRIENDSHIP. FOR KUESU, THESE WERE HAPPY MEMORIES, BUT YUUTO HAS HAD HIS MEMORIES SEALED AWAY FOR A LONG TIME.

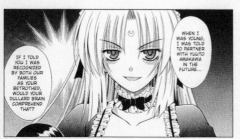

A shocking reunion

WHEN KUESU ASSERTS THEIR ENGAGEMENT, YUUTO RECALLS A BIT OF HIS FORGOTTEN PAST. HE OPENS HIS EYES TO FIND HER KISSING HIM AND REALIZES THAT SHE'S THE GIRL FROM HIS FRAGMENTED MEMORIES.

BECAUSE OF THE PROTECTIVE CHARM GIVEN TO HIM, YUUTO FORGOT ALL ABOUT BOTH MEETING KUESU AND THEIR BETROTHAL. DESPITE THIS, KUESU EMBRACES YUUTO, SAYING, "WHEN I WAS YOUNG, I WAS TOLD TO PARTNER WITH YUUTO AMAKAWA IN MY FUTURE... IF I TOLD YOU I WAS RECOGNIZED BY BOTH FAMILIES AS YOUR BETROTHED, WOULD YOUR DULLARD BRAIN COMPREHEND WHAT I'M SAYING?" THOSE WORDS ALONE BRING BACK MORE MEMORIES TO YUUTO, AND KUESU KISSES HIM. NOT ONCE, BUT TWICE. AFTER THAT DAY, BOTH HIMARI AND SHIZUKU SEEK TO STEAL A KISS FROM YUUTO TOO.

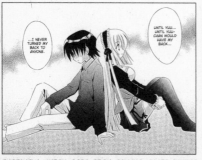

INSTANTLY, KUESU GOES FROM CALLING YUUTO "YUUTO AMAKAWA" TO "YUU-CHAN." WHEN SHE SHOWS HIM THAT FIRST SOFT EXPRESSION SINCE MEETING HIM AGAIN, YUUTO CAN'T HELP HIS HEART BEATING JUST A LITTLE FASTER.

And now they protect each other

KUESU INVITES YUUTO TO CUT ALL TIES WITH AYAKASHI AND FULFILL HIS DEMON-SLAYER DUTIES, BUT HE REFUSES. HOWEVER, DURING THIS EXCHANGE, YUUTO REMEMBERS HOW, WHEN HE WAS A BOY, HE WAS GUNG HO ABOUT DESTROYING DEMONS AND HAD PROMISED THAT HE WOULD ALWAYS HAVE KUESU'S BACK. "...BUT THE ONLY ONES YUU-CHAN EVER PROTECTS ARE THAT CAT AND SNAKE. FRANKLY, I'M DISILLUSIONED," SAYS KUESU. SHE HAD CONTINUED FIGHTING ALL THIS TIME BECAUSE YUUTO'S PROMISE TO HER HAD KEPT HER STRONG.

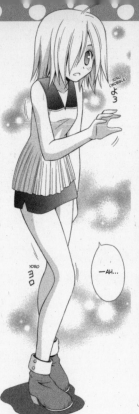

YORO
(MOBILE)

YORO
83

YORO
30

—AH...

Are they drawn to him because he's a demon slayer or because he's so kind?

SINCE YUUTO'S A DEMON SLAYER, HE HAS THE FELINE AYAKASHI HIMARI ACTING AS HIS BODYGUARD. APART FROM HER, THERE ARE MANY AYAKASHI WHO SUDDENLY APPROACH HIM, BUT THEIR AIM IS TO EITHER KILL ALL DEMON SLAYERS, OBSERVE HIM, OR SOMETIMES EVEN SUCK HIS BLOOD... SO THERE REALLY ARE ANY NUMBER OF REASONS.

YUUTO BELIEVES THAT HE AND THESE AYAKASHI WOULD ALL BE ABLE TO GET ALONG AND TALK THINGS OUT. AND WHEN THE SPIRITS THEMSELVES SEE THAT HE'S A DEMON SLAYER WHO HAS TAKEN SUCH A CONTRADICTORY STANCE FROM THE TYPICAL SLAYER, THEY CAN'T HELP BUT BE TAKEN IN. ALL THE SAME, YUUTO'S PEACEFUL DAYS COME TO A CRASHING HALT ON HIS SIXTEENTH BIRTHDAY. LET'S NOW INTRODUCE TO YOU THE AYAKASHI WHO HAVE RATTLED THIS KINDHEARTED DEMON SLAYER'S EVERYDAY LIFE AND THE POWERS THEY POSSESS THAT EXCEED HUMAN KNOWLEDGE!

THE TRUE FACES OF THE SPIRITS that occupy the world of "OMAMORI HIMARI"

I AM NOT SIMPLY A MESSENGER

AYA (A FUGURUMA YOUBI)

THIS IS THE AYAKASHI THAT CAME TO HAND OVER THE CATALOG OF REPLACEMENT SWORDS FOR HIMARI'S YASUTSUNA, WHICH KAYA HAD COMPILED. SHE'S ORIGINALLY A TSUKUMOGAMI FROM A LIBRARY WITH STACKS OF BOOKS. WITH STRAIGHT BANGS AND A WHITE ROBE, SHE HAS A CUTE LOOK TO HER, BUT SHE CAN CARRY A HUGE AMOUNT OF THINGS BY INGESTING THEM. WHEN YUUTO FAILS TO COMFORT HIMARI AFTER SHE TURNED INTO A LITTLE GIRL, AYA AND SHIZUKU HAVE A BIT OF A COMEDIC EXCHANGE BETWEEN EACH OTHER.

WHEN SHE NEEDS TO EXPEL THE CONTENTS OF HER GUT, SHE VOMITS THEM FORTH IN A PROJECTILE MANNER.

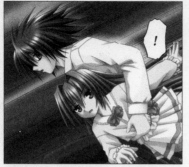

WHEN SHIZUKU WAS IN A PINCH DURING HER FIGHT WITH KUESU, THIS KASHA SWIFTLY RESCUED HER. ISN'T HE SURPRISINGLY CUTE?

HE PROTECTS SHIZUKU FROM THE SHADOWS
KAGETSUKI
(A KASHA)

HE IS ONE OF THE AYAKASHI THAT WORKS WITH SHIZUKU, AND WHEN HE'S NOT IN HIS HUMAN FORM, HE HAS A RATHER GROTESQUE APPEARANCE. ORIGINALLY, HE WOULD APPEAR FROM HELL WHEN MORTAL CRIMINALS DIED AND WOULD STEAL THEIR CORPSES DURING THEIR FUNERALS OR FROM THEIR GRAVES. HE HAS SAVED SHIZUKU AND YUUTO FROM PLENTY OF TIGHT SPOTS AND IS RELATIVELY AMICABLE TOWARD HUMANS.

SHE SUPPORTS HIMARI
KAYA (A ZASHIKI-WARASHI)

AN AYAKASHI SAID TO POSSESS HOUSES AND HELP THEM THRIVE, SHE IS A ZASHIKI-WARASHI. SHE POSSESSED THE AMAKAWA ESTATE IN THE TOWN OF NOIHARA AND HAS KEPT UP THE HOUSE SINCE GRANDPA GEN AND HIS WIFE PASSED AWAY. USING SOMETHING LIKE A FORCE FIELD, A HOME UNDER THE PROTECTION OF A ZASHIKI-WARASHI HAS ENOUGH DEFENSIVE STRENGTH TO RENDER THE HOUSE INDESTRUCTIBLE, EVEN WHEN UNDER ATTACK FROM DAIDABOUSHI (A.K.A. DAIDARABOCCHI). SHE IS VERY ATTACHED TO HIMARI AND IS JEALOUS OF YUUTO.

WHEN YUUTO LEAVES HIMARI TO FIGHT, KAYA SCOLDS HIM SEVERELY.

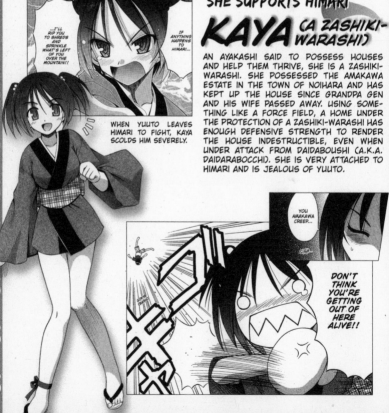

AMAKAWA BLOOD GETS HER HOT

AGEHA
(A HINOENMA)

SHE LOOKS LIKE A BEAUTIFUL BUD-DHIST SAINT, BUT HER INSIDES ARE AS FRIGHTENING AS A DEMON'S. SHE DRINKS THE BLOOD OF THE MEN THAT SHE SEDUCES, SUCKING OUT THEIR VERY LIFE ENERGY AND LEAVING THEM TO DIE. STRONGLY ATTACHED TO PERSONALLY RAISING THE STANDARD OF AYAKASHI, AGEHA FAILS TO END YUUTO'S LIFE. AFTER THAT, SHE TARGETS HIS DEMON-SLAYER BLOOD OVER HIS LIFE.

AGEHA USES A VERY AG-GRESSIVE APPROACH TO MAKE CONTACT WITH YUU-TO. SHE DOESN'T GIVE UP EVEN WHEN REJECTED. IS SHE A CANDIDATE TO BE THE NEW HEROINE...?

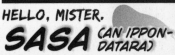

HELLO, MISTER.

SASA (AN IPPON-DATARA)

THE ONE-EYED, ONE-LEGGED AYAKASHI SAID TO ATTACK PEOPLE WHO GET LOST IN THE MOUNTAINS. SHE WORKS WITH AGEHA AND ATTACKS YUUTO AND COMPANY WITH A LASER BEAM THAT SHOOTS OUT OF HER EYE. IN HER HU-MAN FORM, SHE'S A PRETTY BOY WHO GETS MISTAKEN FOR A GIRL. BECAUSE SHE'S USED TO HAVING JUST ONE LEG, SHE CAN'T GET HIS BALANCE QUITE RIGHT AND TRIPS A LOT TO MAKE FOR A GOOD LAUGH. FOR SOME REASON, SHE'S VERY TAKEN WITH RINKO.

IN NOIHARA, SHE FACED OFF AGAINST SHIZUKU AND DROPPED HUGE WOODEN BEAMS FROM THE SKY.

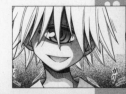

THE LITTLE GIRL WHO EATS AYAKASHI
TAMA-SAN
(THE FAIR-FACED, NINE-TAILED FOX)

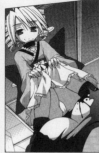

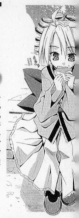

ONE OF THE THREE STRONGEST DEMONS IN JAPAN. IN CHINA, SHE IS KNOWN AS TENJIKU AND IS LEGENDARY IN BOTH COUNTRIES. WHEN SHE TAKES A HUMAN FORM, SHE IS SAID TO BE A WOMAN OF UNSURPASSED BEAUTY, BUT HERE TAMA-SAN APPEARS IN THE FORM OF A GIRL WHO LASHES OUT AT THOSE SHE LIKES. SHE ENJOYS EATING NOT ONLY AYAKASHI, BUT ALSO SWEET TREATS LIKE CREPES.

TAMA-SAN LATCHES RIGHT ON TO HIMARI. BUT SHE SEEMS DISSATISFIED WITH HER TASTE...

HE LURKS IN THE MOUNTAINS
MOUNTAIN SAZAE

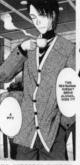

AN AYAKASHI THAT WAS ORIGINALLY A SEA-DWELLING TURBAN SHELL UNTIL IT BECAME SO OLD THAT IT BECAME A DEMON. IT ATTACKS YUUTO AND HIMARI IN THE MOUNTAINS BUT IS DEFEATED BY A SHORT SWORD IMBUED WITH THE LIGHT FERRY POWER.

THOUGH YUUTO DOES HIS UTMOST TO REASON WITH IT, IT DOESN'T UNDERSTAND HUMAN SPEECH AND ATTACKS WITHOUT ANY CHANCE FOR A CONVERSATION.

THE BEING STILL SHROUDED IN MYSTERY
SHUTEN-DOUJI

THIS RESTAURANT DOESN'T SERVE ALCOHOL, DOES IT?

A PITY.

LEGEND HAS IT HE WAS BEHEADED BY THE YASUTSUNA DURING THE HEIAN PERIOD. HE IS ONE OF THE TOP THREE DEMONS IN JAPAN. HE HAS A LAID-BACK AIR ABOUT HIM, BUT HIS ABILITIES ARE STILL UNKNOWN.

HIS CAREFREE EXPRESSION CHANGES WHEN HE SEES THE YASUTSUNA.

DOES THE FACT THAT IT REIGNS SUPREME IN SIZE OVER ALL OTHER AYAKASHI PUT IT AT THE TOP OF THE CLASS?

THE ULTRA-MASSIVE
DAIDARA-BOCCHI

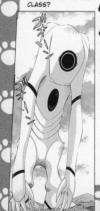

THE AYAKASHI SUMMONED BY AGEHA TO CHALLENGE HIMARI. SOME REGIONS OF JAPAN HAVE LEGENDS THAT TELL OF IT SAVING PEOPLE, AND IT SEEMS TO HAVE A GENERALLY WELL-MEANING NATURE.

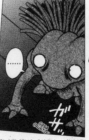

......

RELATIVELY SMALL, HIMARI SPOTS IT ON THE ROOF AND PROMPTLY SLICES IT IN TWO.

HE TARGETS HUMANS IN ANGUISH
MAKURA-GAESHI

FEEDING ON HUMAN DREAMS, THIS TROUBLEMAKING AYAKASHI WILL SHOW ITS VICTIM WHATEVER DREAM HE OR SHE WISHES, EVENTUALLY SAPPING THEM OF THEIR LIFE FORCE. HE POSSESSED RINKO BECAUSE SHE DREAMT OF HAVING YUUTO ALL TO HERSELF.

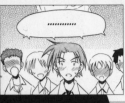

....

The other folks who can be found at the school Yuuto, Rinko, and Himari attend. Both their classmates and teachers alike are independent and arguably have even more presence than an average ayakashi...what do you think!?

The people of Yuuto's school

TOURYOU HIGH

Introducing your queen...!!

Now to crown the winner of this year's Miss Touryou beauty contest!

Lizlet L. Chelsie-chan!!

The tea maid at Café Relish in the Iriya Shopping Center—

11 6 18 7

TOURYOU HIGH IS THE COED HIGH SCHOOL WHERE YUUTO AND RINKO STUDY. TO GET AN IDEA OF JUST HOW LIBERAL IT IS, THE SCHOOL'S ART DEPARTMENT TAKES STUDENTS OUT OF TOWN ON SKETCHING EXCURSIONS. IN THE AUTUMN, THE TOURYOU FESTIVAL IS HELD, AND ONE OF ITS MANY HIGHLIGHTS IS THE MISS TOURYOU BEAUTY CONTEST. THIS YEAR'S WINNER WAS LIZ, SO EVEN THOSE WHO AREN'T STUDENTS AT THE SCHOOL CAN COMPETE, IT SEEMS.

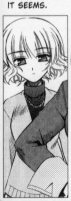

Soft-spoken Yuuko-chan

YUUKO AKUTSU

SHE NORMALLY HIDES IN KISARAGI-SENSEI'S SHADOW AS SHE HAS A BARELY THERE SORT OF PRESENCE, BUT IN REALITY SHE IS THE VERY BEAUTIFUL ART TEACHER. SHE HAS HER SHARE OF FANS WHO LONG FOR HER QUIETLY.

PERHAPS HER QUIET NATURE IS ONE OF HER MORE CHARMING POINTS!?

Yuuto's classmate

TAIZOU MASAKI

YUUTO'S BEST FRIEND CAN'T HELP BEING A TYPICAL HIGH SCHOOL BOY AND HAS GOTTEN HIS SHARE OF BRUISES FOR THE WAY HE APPROACHES HIMARI, RINKO, AND THE OTHER GIRLS. HE GOT A NOSEBLEED OVER THEIR SWIMSUITS AT THE BEACH, AND HIS PERVERTED NATURE WAS HOW HE LANDED HIMSELF THE JOB OF EMCEE FOR THE MISS TOURYOU BEAUTY CONTEST. THIS YOUNG MAN JUST CAN'T HIDE HIS HEALTHY LIBIDO.

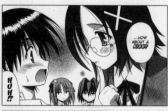

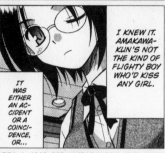

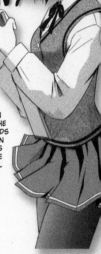

Still without a real name
CLASS PRESIDENT

RINKO'S BEST FRIEND AND THE PRESIDENT OF YUUTO'S CLASS. THOUGH SHE'S NOWHERE NEAR HIMARI'S OR LIZ'S SIZE, SHE HAS A PRETTY AMPLE RACK AND ATTRACTED PLENTY OF ATTENTION FROM THE MALE CONTINGENT AT THE BEACH. SHE IS RINKO'S EVER-CONSTANT CONFIDANTE WHEN IT COMES TO MATTERS OF THE HEART. SHE MAINLY RECOMMENDS RADICAL ADVICE, LIKE TAKING AN ACTIVE ROLE IN MAKING THINGS HAPPEN AND PLACING LITTLE EMPHASIS ON SUPERFICIAL LOOKS, ET CETERA.

WITH A NOSE FOR INVESTIGATION, THE CLASS PRESIDENT RESEARCHES KUESU'S PAST AND SHARES IT WITH YUUTO.

The out-there female teacher
SAE KISARAGI

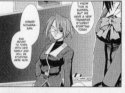

YUUTO'S HOMEROOM TEACHER. SHE POSSESSES A DUO OF FORMIDABLE WEAPONS (?)—GLASSES AND BIG BREASTS—AND YET DRESSES IN TIGHT CLOTHING THAT EMPHASIZES HER RACK, PRACTICALLY DARING THE MALE STUDENTS TO LOOK. SHE SEEMS TO BE A REGULAR AT THE MAID CAFÉ WHERE LIZ WORKS AND IS KNOWN TO ENJOY A CUP OF TEA WITH A CIGARETTE.

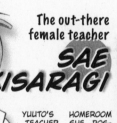

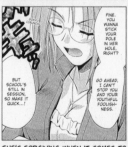

SHE'S FORGIVING WHEN IT COMES TO HEALTHY SEXUALITY, BUT SHE GETS MAD WHEN "THIS" AND "THAT" GOES ON DURING CLASS.

WHO ARE THE TWELVE DEMON-SLAYER FAMILIES!?

These important key words keep showing up in OMAMORI HIMARI: demon slayer. We're going to delve into the true identities behind those who are so feared by the ayakashi!

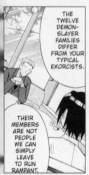

THE AMAKAWA ARE A DEMON-SLAYER FAMILY, BUT BECAUSE THEY CHOSE TO MAKE A PACT WITH HIMARI'S ANCESTORS, THEY WERE REVILED BY THEIR PEERS.

THE TWELVE DEMON-SLAYER FAMILIES DIFFER FROM YOUR TYPICAL EXORCISTS.

THEIR MEMBERS ARE NOT PEOPLE WE CAN SIMPLY LEAVE TO RUN RAMPANT.

DUE TO THE TREMENDOUS POWER THEY POSSESS, IF A DEMON-SLAYER FAMILY WAS TO ABANDON THEIR DUTY, THEY COULD BECOME THREATS.

DEMON EXTERMINATORS WHO HAVE PROTECTED THE HUMAN WORLD SINCE ANCIENT TIMES

A DEMON SLAYER IS A PERSON WHO POSSESSES UNIQUE POWERS AND VANQUISHES EVIL AYAKASHI THAT DO PEOPLE HARM. THE "TWELVE DEMON-SLAYER FAMILIES" REFERS TO THE BLOODLINES OF HUMANS WHO POSSESS PARTICULARLY STRONG POWERS COMPARED TO THE AVERAGE DEMON EXTERMINATOR OR DEMON HUNTER.

THE FIRST DEMON SLAYERS WERE ESTABLISHED DURING THE HEIAN PERIOD, AND THEY'VE FOUGHT AYAKASHI IN EXCHANGE FOR HIGH RANK AND VAST FORTUNES EVER SINCE. HOWEVER, AS TIMES CHANGED, THERE WERE FEWER OPPORTUNITIES FOR THEM TO MAKE USE OF THEIR ABILITIES. SOME CLANS WERE COMPLETELY LOST DURING THE GREAT WAR, WHILE OTHERS SEALED AWAY THEIR SPECIAL POWERS AND ASSIMILATED INTO GENERAL SOCIETY. AS A RESULT, THEY EXIST TODAY IN A REMARKABLY DECLINED STATE COMPARED TO THEIR GOLDEN AGE.

EVEN SO, THE FEW REMAINING DEMON-SLAYER FAMILIES THAT ARE ACTIVE STILL STRIKE FEAR INTO THE HEARTS OF AYAKASHI AT JUST THE SOUND OF THEIR NAMES. THAT IS WHY YUUTO, WHO HAS NOT YET COME INTO HIS POWERS FULLY, IS BEING TARGETED FOR ANNIHILATION. NOW THAT BIGGER AND STRONGER ENEMIES HAVE CONFRONTED HIM, WHAT WILL YUUTO CHOOSE TO DO AS BOTH A DEMON SLAYER AND THE LAST LIVING DESCENDANT OF THE AMAKAWA FAMILY...?

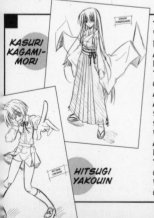

KASURI KAGAMIMORI

HITSUGI YAKOUIN

THOUGH THEY ARE CALLED THE "TWELVE FAMILIES," THERE ARE CURRENTLY ONLY THREE CLANS RECOGNIZED AS ACTIVE IN THIS DAY AND AGE. EVEN INCLUDING THOSE FAMILIES WHOSE STATUS IS UNKNOWN, THE TOTAL NUMBER OF DEMON-SLAYER FAMILIES STILL ONLY AMOUNTS TO SIX. APART FROM YUUTO AND KUESU, ONLY TWO OTHER ACTIVE SLAYERS ARE CURRENTLY KNOWN: KASURI KAGAMIMORI, THE SHRINE MAIDEN WHO POSSESSES THE "BEAST EYES," AND HITSUGI YAKOUIN, THE GIRL WITH LIGHTNING-FAST COGNITIVE SKILLS. THEY BOTH SEEM TO BE RATHER QUIRKY CHARACTERS, BUT IT WILL BE WORTHWHILE TO SEE WHAT THEY'RE REALLY CAPABLE OF.

WHAT OTHER DEMON SLAYERS ARE THERE BESIDES YUUTO AND KUESU?

1st Rank Tsuchimikado Family

AN ESOTERIC COSMOLOGY FAMILY TRAINED IN THE ABE STYLE AND RENOWNED AS THE STRONGEST DEMON-SLAYER FAMILY. UNLIKE THE JINGUUJI, THEY'RE SHROUDED IN MYSTERY TO HIDE THEIR ACTIVITIES.

◆CURRENT STATUS—ACTIVE

2nd Rank Kamizakura Family

THIS FAMILY USES ANCIENT SHINTO CHARMS AND CURSES. AFTER THE GREAT WAR, THEY SAW THEIR SUPERHUMAN POWERS AS A THREAT AND SEALED THEM AWAY. AFTER THAT, THEY FADED INTO OBSCURITY.

◆CURRENT STATUS—UNKNOWN

3rd Rank Kagamimori Family

THIS FAMILY MAKES USE OF ANCIENT SHINTO MIRROR-GUARD PROCEDURES AND MAGIC SEALING. THEY ARE THE ONLY FAMILY WHO DOES NOT "EXTERMINATE" THEIR ADVERSARIES SO MUCH AS "SEAL" THEM AWAY. ONLY A SHRINE MAIDEN WITH "BEAST EYES" CAN HEAD THE FAMILY.

◆CURRENT STATUS—ACTIVE

4th Rank Kogetsukyou Family

SPRUNG FROM THE ANCIENT FORBIDDEN ARTS, THIS FAMILY SPECIALIZED IN MORTAL CURSES AND TREATMENTS. THEY'RE ONE OF TWO FAMILIES THAT WERE PART OF THE GERMAN AHNENERBE SOCIETY.

◆CURRENT STATUS—DECEASED

5th Rank Houjou Family

THIS FAMILY COULD MANIPULATE ELECTROMAGNETIC WAVES, BUT SINCE THE CONCEPT OF ELECTRICITY IS A FAIRLY RECENT ONE, THEY INSTEAD CALLED THEMSELVES "THUNDER MASTERS." AT THE START OF THE SHOWA PERIOD, A MYSTERIOUS EXPLOSION DECIMATED BOTH THEIR ESTATE AND ALL THE MEMBERS OF THE FAMILY. HOWEVER, THERE IS SPECULATION THAT THEY BROUGHT ABOUT THEIR OWN DEMISE THROUGH RESEARCH AND DEVELOPMENT GONE WRONG.

◆CURRENT STATUS—DECEASED

6th Rank Amakawa Family

THEY POSSESS THE LIGHT FERRY, WHICH CAN AUGMENT AN OBJECT'S GIVEN POWER AS WELL AS SEAL AWAY MAGIC POWERS. THOUGH THEY RANK SIXTH, THEY WERE LOOKED DOWN UPON BY THE OTHER FAMILIES FOR THEIR ASSOCIATION WITH AYAKASHI, LIKE HIMARI'S ANCESTORS. THOUGH THEY LOST THE OTHER FAMILIES' TRUST AND RESPECT BECAUSE OF THE ASSOCIATION, THEIR REPUTATION WAS MENDED AFTER THE WAR WHEN THEY CAME TO BE SEEN AS MODEL EXAMPLES OF THE COEXISTENCE BETWEEN AYAKASHI AND HUMANS. THE FAMILY'S POWER IS INHERITED THROUGH THE BOYS.

◆CURRENT STATUS—UNKNOWN

7th Rank Karasu Family

THIS FAMILY ONLY BATTLED DEMONS THROUGH SWORDSMANSHIP. AT THE HEIGHT OF THE EDO PERIOD, THEY CHALLENGED THE TEMPORARILY REVIVED "NINE-TAILS," BUT WERE OVERWHELMED AND PERISHED.

◆CURRENT STATUS—DECEASED

8th Rank Jibashiri Family

THIS FAMILY HARBORED THE ENERGY OF THE EARTH WITHIN THEIR BODIES AND BOASTED SUPERNATURAL STRENGTH. IT IS SAID THAT THEY WOULD ACCEPT ANY COMMISSION SO LONG AS IT HAD AN AWARD WAITING FOR THEM AT THE END. THEY JOINED THE GREAT WAR AS LOWER-RANKED OFFICERS AND DIED ON THE MAINLAND. THEY ARE AN EXTINCT FAMILY LINE, THOUGH THERE IS SPECULATION THAT A TINY OFFSHOOT OF THE FAMILY SURVIVES.

◆CURRENT STATUS—DECEASED

9th Rank Homura Family

THIS FAMILY COULD FREELY MANIPULATE FIRE AT WILL. THEY WERE THE OTHER FAMILY AFFILIATED WITH THE GERMAN AHNENERBE SOCIETY DURING THE GREAT WAR. THE TWO AFFILIATED HOUSES BOTH DIED DURING THE BATTLE AND BECAME EXTINCT.

◆CURRENT STATUS—DECEASED

10th Rank Hiiragi Family

THE FAMILY THAT CONTROLLED WIND AND ALSO EXCELLED IN MARTIAL ARTS. AT THE START OF UPHEAVAL BETWEEN THE WARRING STATES, THEY WERE TO CLOSE THE GATES TO HELL WITH THE HELP OF THE OTHER FAMILIES, THOUGH THEY ENDED UP LOSING THE HEAD OF THEIR FAMILY TO THE DARKNESS. AFTER THAT, THEY QUIETLY RETIRED WITHOUT PRODUCING ANY POWERFUL OFFSPRING.

◆CURRENT STATUS—DECEASED

11th Rank Yakouin Family

THIS FAMILY CAN SEE INTO THE FUTURE AND PROCESS INFORMATION VERY QUICKLY. HOWEVER, IT CAN CAUSE SENSORY OVERLOAD FROM THE LOSS OF BRAIN CELLS, RESULTING IN DEATH, SO THEY KEEP THEIR DEMON-SLAYER DUTIES TO A MINIMUM. THE CURRENT HEAD OF THE FAMILY IS HITSUGI YAKOUIN, A PRETTY LITTLE GIRL WHO IS ACTIVE AS A DETECTIVE.

◆CURRENT STATUS—UNKNOWN

12th Rank Jinguuji Family

THEIR ORIGINS UNCLEAR, THIS FAMILY CASTS SPELLS AND USES MAGIC. THEY WERE INDUCTED INTO THE TWELVE FAMILIES FOR THEIR EXTERMINATING ABILITIES, BUT THEIR METHODS WERE SEEN AS HERETICAL. THEY EVENTUALLY TURNED TO WESTERN DARK ARTS. THEY HAVE THE MOST MAGICAL ABILITY OUT OF ALL THE FAMILIES NOW, THOUGH THAT POWER IS ONLY PASSED DOWN THROUGH THE GIRLS.

◆CURRENT STATUS—ACTIVE

WHAT BOY WOULDN'T GET HARD OVER THIS!? IT'S HIMARI SNEAKING INTO HIS ROOM FOR SOME ACTION AT NIGHT!

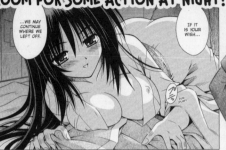

...WE MAY CONTINUE WHERE WE LEFT OFF.

IF IT IS YOUR WISH...

"IF IT IS YOUR WISH..." BUT WHAT DOES THAT MEAN? OH, NOI-HARA-SAN. HOW CAN YUUTO CALL HIMSELF A MAN WHEN HE GETS SO FLUSTERED OVER THIS!? PATHETIC!

IN ADDITION TO THE DYNAMIC DEVELOPMENTS EVERY FEW PAGES IN THIS SERIES, ANOTHER VERY APPEALING PART OF *OMAMORI HIMARI* IS THAT YOU'RE BOUND TO RUN ACROSS SOME RISQUÉ SCENES. SURE, IT'S TYPICALLY ONLY YUUTO HAVING RUN-INS WITH THESE MORE AROUSING, SHALL WE SAY, SITUATIONS, BUT AS A REPRESENTATIVE FOR HEALTHY YOUNG MEN THE WORLD OVER, TAIZOU MASAKI-SENSEI HAS VOLUNTEERED TO LEND A HAND (CHA!) AND ACT AS A GUIDE TO THIS SIDE OF THE OMAHIMA UNIVERSE! FROM PANTY SHOTS TO VIRTUALLY X-RATED (?) TABLEAUX, TAIZOU'S KEEN EYE HAS SELECTED THE GIRLS' MOST FANTASTIC EFFORTS!

YOU CAN'T IGNORE SHIZUKU'S KNACK FOR SNEAK PEEKS.

HOW LEWD...

...AND DIRTY... YOU KNOW.

I'M NO PEDO, BUT JUST LOOK AT THIS SHOT OF SHIZUKU-CHAN. ONE SMALL GLANCE REVEALS IT ALL...

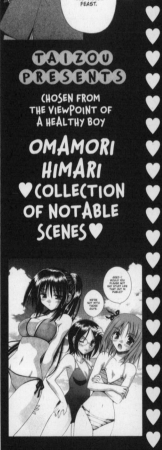

GETTING TO ENJOY AND APPRECIATE A WHOLE THRONG OF CUTE GIRLS IS ANY SANE AND HEALTHY BOY'S DEEPEST DESIRE.

I'M JUST GONNA ENJOY THIS VISUAL FEAST.

TAIZOU PRESENTS

CHOSEN FROM THE VIEWPOINT OF A HEALTHY BOY

OMAMORI HIMARI ♥ COLLECTION OF NOTABLE SCENES ♥

JEEZ~! WOULD YOU PLEASE NOT SAY STUFF LIKE THAT OUT IN PUBLIC?!

WE'RE NOT WITH THOSE GUYS.

RINKO EXPRESSES HERSELF IN A WAY THAT GOES BEYOND CHILDHOOD FRIENDSHIP...

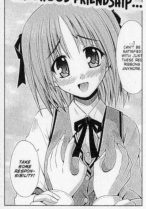

...I CAN'T BE SATISFIED WITH JUST THESE RED RIBBONS ANYMORE.

TAKE SOME RESPON-SIBILITY!

WHY DOES YUUTO GET ALL THE ATTEN-TION...? STILL, IT'S HARD TO BELIEVE THE TOMBOY KUZAKI WOULD ACTUALLY HAVE THOUGHTS LIKE THESE.

FAR FROM THE EXPRESSIONLES TAMA-SAN IS...

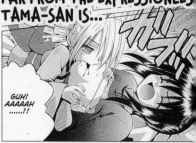

GUH! AAAAAH ......!!

WITH HER EVER-DEADPAN FACE ON, TAMA-SAN TAKES A BIG BITE OUT OF NOIHARA-SAN'S PLUMPER PARTS. IT'S LIKE IT MAKES NO DIFFERENCE WHETHER IT'S A HUMAN OR AN AYAKASHI...

HAS HE LOST ALL SENSES!? HIMARI OFFERS A REWARD.

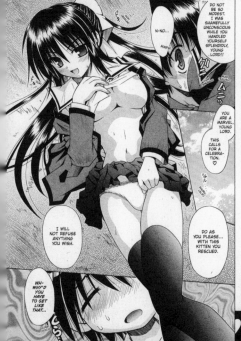

N-NO...

DO NOT BE SO MODEST. I WAS SHAMEFULLY UNCONSCIOUS WHILE YOU HANDLED YOURSELF SPLENDIDLY, YOUNG LORD!!

YOU ARE A MARVEL, YOUNG LORD.

THIS CALLS FOR A CELEBRATION. ♡

I WILL NOT REFUSE ANYTHING YOU WISH.

DO AS YOU PLEASE... WITH THIS KITTEN YOU RESCUED.

WH-WHY'D YOU HAVE TO GET LIKE THAT...

IF AGEHA SAID THAT ...TO ME!

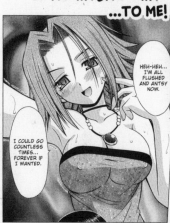

HEH-HEH... I'M ALL FLUSHED AND ANTSY NOW.

I COULD GO COUNTLESS TIMES... FOREVER IF I WANTED.

"I'M ALL FLUSHED AND ANTSY NOW." WOW, IF SOMEBODY SAID THAT TO ME... AND HOW ABOUT THAT PART WHERE SHE GOES, "I COULD GO COUNTLESS TIMES...FOREVER IF I WANTED." YUUTO IS GETTING THE LONG END OF THE STICK WAY TOO MANY TIMES, PERIOD!

THIS SCENE REQUIRES NO COMMENT! NOT ONLY ARE YOU GETTING ALL SORTS OF EXCITING PEEKS, BUT SEEING NOIHARA-SAN ACTUALLY BREAKING OUT IN A SWEAT... JUMP HER, YUUTO. A REAL MAN WOULD CHARGE FULL SPEED AHEAD!

MORNING

YUUTO WAKES UP WITH SOMETHING SOFT AND SQUISHY IN HIS HAND. I TAKE THAT BACK. HE'S TOTALLY MANHANDLING HIMARI WHILE SHE PRETENDS TO BE DEAD ASLEEP!?

NOON

THE YOUNG MASTER REACTS BETTER THROUGH STIMULATION, DOES HE NOT?

IN THAT CASE...

THOUGH HE'S UP AGAINST A WALL, YUUTO'S EYES ARE MET WITH SOMETHING VERY PLEASING. UNBECOMING OF A MASTER-SERVANT RELATIONSHIP, HIMARI FIRST INVADES HIS PERSONAL SPACE AND THEN SNARES HIM WITH HER SMOOTH TONGUE.

NIGHT

PHOOO...?

HIMARI LOSES HER SENSES THANKS TO A SECRET PILL THAT INCLUDES CATNIP-LIKE INGREDIENTS. NOW THAT SHE SEES YUUTO AS HER PREY, WILL HE BE CONSUMED BY HER?

UP TO THIS POINT, PRETTY MUCH THE ONLY GIRL IN YUUTO'S LIFE WAS RINKO. THEN HIMARI JOINED THEIR RANKS, SHIZUKU APPEARED OUT OF NOWHERE, AND LIZ BEFRIENDED HIM. ADD TO THAT OTHER BEAUTIES LIKE KUESU AND AGEHA, AND SUDDENLY YUUTO'S STARTING TO LOOK A LOT LIKE A KING WITH HIS OWN HAREM! IT'S ENOUGH TO MAKE ANY GUY GREEN WITH ENVY... AND MAYBE A LITTLE SCARED TOO...

MORNING,
NOON,
AND
NIGHT,
HE'S WITH A
KNOCK-OUT!

YUUTO AMAKAWA'S
"Girl Trouble"
ALBUM

IN THE PARK

YUUTO ACCIDENTALLY GETS A GOOD LOOK AT LIZ'S WHITE PANTIES. WASN'T HE SUPPOSED TO BE UNDERGOING SPECIAL COMBAT TRAINING IN THE PARK...?

IN THE CAFÉ

EVEN THOUGH RINKO WAS CLOSING IN ON HIM, ANOTHER TONGUE MAKES A REACH FOR YUUTO. ...AND THAT'S HOW HE ENDS UP IN A DEEP, LONG (LITERALLY!) KISS WITH SHIZUKU. I THINK SHE'S HOOKED HIM!

ON THE ROAD

ON THE WAY HOME, KIESU SUDDENLY APPEARS, DECLARES HERSELF YUUTO'S BETROTHED, AND THEN LAYS ONE ON HIM, AND THE SECOND ONE'S A FULL-ON FRENCH KISS AT THAT. YUUTO'S COMPLETELY OVERWHELMED BY ALL THIS.

ON THE MOUNTAIN

IN ORDER TO HEAL YUUTO AFTER HE WAS HURT AND GOT KNOCKED OUT, SHIZUKU HOLDS HIM IN A NAKED EMBRACE. SHE'S DRIPPING WET, BUT SHE'S NOT JUST DOING THIS FOR FUN. THIS IS A RESPECTED METHOD OF TREATMENT.

...I'M GOING TO SEAL THE GASH...

HOLD HIM UP FOR ME, YOU KNOW.

I SUP- POSE I... HAVE NO CHOICE.

IN THE LIVING ROOM

...RD.

"J-JUST A LITTLE PECK ON THE CHEEK...WILL DO, IF THAT IS ALL RIGHT?" YUUTO'S HEART FEELS A PANG WHEN HE HEARS HIMARI SAY THAT. AND FOR ONCE HE ACTUALLY TAKES SOME INITIATIVE...

AT THE FESTIVAL

YUUTO'S TOUCHING MY BREAST.

WHAT DO I DO? WHAT DO I DO? HE'S GOT ME PINNED DOWN.

FALLING, HE ENDS UP ON THE GROUND ALONG WITH HER, BUT THE SIDE TO REVEAL SOME FLESH. HE AND RINKO STILL RE- MAIN SIMPLY FRIENDS. ...TO KEEP RINKO FROM TRIPPING AND EVEN AFTER CATCHING A GLIMPSE OF HER YUKATA HIKED TO

Himari, I am an ayakashi too. I am a cute cat... ♡

IN VOLUME 1, WHERE THE CURTAIN IS RAISED ON OUR STORY, HIMARI MAKES HER ENTRANCE IMMEDIATELY. YUUTO AND RINKO ARE THROWN OFF BY THIS SUDDEN EVENT AND QUICKLY REALIZE THAT THINGS WILL NEVER BE QUITE THE SAME. HOWEVER, WHEN THEY GO TO THE MOUNTAIN AND THEN THE BEACH, YUUTO AND HIMARI BEGIN TO CLOSE THE GAP OF UNFAMILIARITY BETWEEN THEM. THAT'S WHEN OUR NEXT AYAKASHI, SHIZUKU, SHOWS UP! THE SITUATION'S A LITTLE TOUCH AND GO, BUT EITHER WAY, YUUTO FINDS HIMSELF SURROUNDED BY GIRLS (AYAKASHI INCLUDED)...

WHEN YUUTO WITNESSES HIMARI'S HIDDEN, VIOLENT SIDE COMING THROUGH, HE'S LEFT FEELING A LITTLE UN-EASY.

AND AMIDST THE FRENZY OF THY BLOOMING, LET THY BLOSSOMS SCATTER FLEETINGLY IN THE WIND!!

BLOOM WILDLY!!

YOU'RE JUST SOME MONSTER, SO DON'T GO STICKING YOUR NOSE INTO OUR BUSINESS!!

HOW DARE YOU TALK TO ME LIKE THAT! YOU'RE A CAT!

HIMARI AND THE OTHER GIRLS NURSE YUUTO BACK TO HEALTH AFTER HE PASSES OUT IN THE TUB. AFTER GETTING AN UP CLOSE AND PERSONAL LOOK AT THE GOODS, NATURALLY (HA!).

GYAAUGH!!

THEY MOST CER-TAINLY DID LOOK.

RINKO GETS MAD AT HIMARI FOR SUDDENLY SHOWING UP AND TRYING TO HOG YUUTO. THAT'S WHY SHE CAN'T CONTROL HERSELF AND YELLS THESE BITING REMARKS...

Matra's COMMENT

Since this was my first serialization in a regular magazine, I concerned myself more with attacking with what I'm best at rather than trying to overextend myself. By Chapter 3, I already had my away-from-school episode and heard a lot of teasing, like "Isn't this supposed to be a school-based story?" (ha!). The cover image was the first I'd ever done, and I tried to make it hook as many readers as possible (heh!)! That's why I drew Himari with the kind of gentle smile you never see in the story itself. And she also shows her panties, which she typically hides under her Japanese garb. It really tore down the norms of the character.

Table of Contents

A bodyguard has her pride as a bodyguard. I need no pity.

WHEN SHIZUKU STARTS TO DOMINATE THE CHORES IN THE AMAKAWA HOUSEHOLD, HIMARI THINKS TO APPLY HERSELF TO A PART-TIME JOB. THAT'S WHERE WE MEET OUR NEWEST CHARACTER: THE WELL-ENDOWED MAID LIZ. THERE'S ALSO AN EPISODE THAT EXPLORES RINKO'S AND YUUTO'S CHILDHOOD, AND YUUTO LEARNS MORE ABOUT THE SECRETS OF THE DEMON SLAYERS WHEN HE VISITS NOIHARA, WHERE HE GREW UP. OVERALL, THERE ARE A LOT OF SCENES YOU DON'T WANT TO MISS. OF COURSE, THERE ARE ALSO JUST AS MANY SCENES ESSENTIAL FOR THEIR SEX APPEAL ALONE!

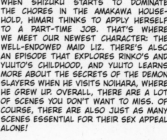

OMAMORI HIMARI 2

RINKO ACTUALLY SCORES A WIN AGAINST HIMARI, WHEN RINKO MEANS BUSINESS, IS SHE MORE FRIGHTENING THAN AN AYAKASHI!?

GOOD THING THIS SHRINE IS ENEMY TERRITORY FOR HER...

I...I WON...!

RINKO...?

WHY IS HIMARI KNOCKED OUT?

LIZ'S TRUE FORM, A TEACUP. IT'S A TREASURE THAT GIVES OFF A HIGH-CLASS VIBE.

IT'S PART OF A SET, BUT THIS TEACUP IS AN OLD PIECE FROM ENGLAND.

I FOUND IT AT AN ANTIQUE SHOP.

WHAT IS THIS RED SUB-STANCE...?

YOUNG LORD... WHAT IS THAT PRO-TRUDING FROM YOUR BACK...?

IN AN ATTEMPT TO SAVE HIMARI, YUUTO THROWS HIMSELF IN FRONT OF AGEHA...!

Matra's COMMENT

Since it was Volume 2, I drew two characters with two panty shots (ha!) for the cover. It was around this time that I decided to add Shizuku and Liz, and even have a chapter devoted to Rinko for the sake of throwing a little variety into the story mix. In Chapter 10, we enter the "Noihara Arc" (also called the "Twilight Arc"), where we see a little more of the workings of the Amakawa demon-slayer family. In any case, the story starts to pick up its development pace here. We also see Himari's bloodthirsty mode and the Light Ferry for the first time. And I shamelessly added a bunch of gimmicks to entice the readers' interest even more.

Table of Contents

The Young Lord chose to kiss me of his own accord, see?

NOW THAT YUUTO KNOWS ABOUT THE DEMON-SLAYER POWERS RESIDING WITHIN HIS BODY, HE'S AT A LOSS. NOT WANTING TO CAUSE ANY TROUBLE FOR HIMARI, HE TRIES TO UNDERGO SOME SPECIAL TRAINING BUT GETS A LITTLE MORE THAN HE BARGAINED FOR BY WAY OF FEMALE ATTENTION. WHILE HE'S CONCENTRATING ON THESE OTHER THINGS, ANOTHER DEMON SLAYER NAMED KUESU APPEARS AND PROCLAIMS HERSELF YUUTO'S BETROTHED. IN MORE WAYS THAN ONE, THE FIGHT INTENSIFIES, AND YUUTO HAS NO TIME TO COLLECT HIS WITS. THERE'S ALSO A SPECIAL COLLECTION OF FOUR-PANEL COMICS YOU WON'T WANT TO MISS!

IN AN ATTEMPT TO SUMMON BACK YUUTO'S MEMORIES OF HER, KUESU STEALS A KISS. AND HIMARI IS THOROUGHLY SHOCKED!

SHIZUKU PURPOSELY GETS NAKED TO HEAL YUUTO. AND IT'S ALL FOR THE REASON SHE STATES BELOW...

DON'T MAKE ME ADMIT SOMETHING SO EMBARRASSING OUT LOUD, YOU KNOW...

IT MADE ME...... FEEL SO GOOD......

...MEOW

BOOOO (STARES)

ほ!!

WHAT WAS SUPPOSED TO BE A "PECK ON THE CHEEK" BECOMES A KISS ON THE MOUTH. HIMARI'S SO CUTE WHEN SHE GETS FLUSTERED OVER UNEXPECTED DEVELOPMENTS.

Matra's COMMENT

For Volume 3, I drew three characters with three panty shots on the cover (ha!). We take a break from the countryside arc and enter the "Kuesu Arc." As a face from Yuuto's past, Kuesu takes on the role of Himari's biggest rival (even though she already made an appearance in the illustration I did for Dragon Age's announcement of this new series). I had originally planned for *OMAMORI HIMARI* to end at six volumes, so Kuesu's appearance was supposed to be a turning point. But...following that, I got a request from the editorial department to extend the length of the series!!

Table of Contents

Young Lord... What have you done to me?

OMAMORI HIMARI COMIC DIGEST

YUUTO IS STARTLED BY KUESU, WHO COMES ONTO THE SCENE LIKE A STORM. AND HIMARI, SHIZUKU, AND RINKO GET SWEPT UP IN THE TURMOIL TOO. IT SPURS ALL THE LADIES TO START THINKING ABOUT THEIR RELATIONSHIP WITH YUUTO AND STEPS THEY CAN TAKE TO ADVANCE IT. HOWEVER, KUESU'S NOT ABOUT TO GET LEFT IN THE DUST EITHER. AFTER ALL, YUUTO IS A SIGNIFICANT PRESENCE IN HER LIFE. AND AS IT SEEMS KUESU'S GOT THE UPPER HAND IN EVERY WAY, THE LAST THING WE SEE IS HIMARI'S BODY UNDERGOING A STRANGE TRANSFORMATION...

OMAMORI HIMARI 4

I'M SAYING!! I'LL TAKE CARE OF ANY SEXUAL DESIRES YOU MAY BE INADVERTENTLY DIRECTING TOWARD THOSE AYAKASHI...!

UH, WHAT ON EARTH ARE YOU GOING ON ABOUT...?

JUST WHEN KUESU AND YUUTO WERE STARTING TO WARM UP TO EACH OTHER, SHE GETS FLUSTERED AND BLURTS THAT OUT.....!

BECAUSE SHE DOESN'T HAVE THE POWER TO FIGHT AYAKASHI, RINKO FIGURES THE BEST SHE CAN DO FOR YUUTO IS GIVE HIM HIS "EVERYDAY LIFE" JUST AS IT'S ALWAYS BEEN.

FORGIVE ME, YASU-TSUNA...

MY SWORD GIVEN TO ME BY GRANDPA GEN.

HIMARI LOSES THE BELOVED SWORD WITH WHICH SHE HAS FOUGHT SO LONG. IT WAS GIVEN TO HER BY GRANDPA GEN.

Matra's COMMENT

Having reached Volume 4, I drew four characters with four panty—that would have been impossible (heh!). Since the series was now slated to run longer, it was at this stage that a turning point took place, shifting the story into one that would appeal to a broader audience. Kuesu appears, and the characters are forced to reevaluate their own positions. At the same time, instead of focusing on Yuuto's lost memories, his main concern becomes how he will choose to live his life hereafter. I'll admit that all these changes make things a little chaotic, so that's why I threw in the playful episode about Himari turning into a little girl.

Table of Contents

> I am the blade that shall slaughter all enemies, the shield that shall deflect any disaster.

JUST WHEN HIMARI'S SHRUNKEN IN SIZE AND IS UNABLE TO FIGHT, WHO SHOULD MAKE AN ENTRANCE BUT THE GANG'S EARLIER AYAKASHI OPPONENTS AGEHA AND SASA!? AS EXPECTED, AGEHA IS STILL AFTER YUUTO'S LIFE...BUT NOW IN ANOTHER EXTREMELY SURPRISING WAY! FOLLOWING A LULL IN THE ACTION, TAMA-SAN AND SHUTEN-DOUJI, THE MOST DANGEROUS ENEMIES HIMARI AND COMPANY HAVE YET ENCOUNTERED, TAKE THE STAGE...!

THE SECOND HALF OF THIS VOLUME FEATURES A BONUS: MATRA-SENSEI'S DEBUT WORK FOR A REGULAR MANGA ANTHOLOGY! DON'T MISS THE STORY OF THESE DELIGHTFUL LADIES EITHER, Y'HEAR?

OMAMORI HIMARI 5

IT'S AS THOUGH HIMARI'S WORDS ARE HINTING AT DEVELOPMENTS TO COME....

SO THAT EVEN AFTER YOU MUST RELINQUISH YOUR VALUES, YOU HAVE NO REGRETS.

ENJOY THE PRESENT WHILE YOU ARE ABLE.

I WENT OUT OF MY WAY TO FIX YOUR SWORD FOR YOU!

THANKS TO KUESU, HIMARI'S LOST YASUTSUNA IS RESTORED, ALONG WITH HER RESOLVE TO FIGHT.

IF YOU EVER MEET THOSE GOONS AGAIN...

...PUT AT LEAST ONE OF THEM TO DEATH WITH THIS!!

WITH A LIGHT, FERRY-INFUSED SHORT SWORD, THE BODYGUARD HIMARI MAKES A FULL COMEBACK!

SO YOU ARE MORE POWERFUL NOW THAT YOU HAVE SIPPED THE BLOOD OF THE YOUNG LORD...

BUT I HAVE COME EQUIPPED WITH THE YOUNG LORD'S INTENTIONS.

Matra's COMMENT

Who would have thought that Ageha of all people would make it onto the cover (ha)! Volume 5 also hit the shelves with the announcement that OMAMORI HIMARI would be made into an anime. "Commence Operation!" was originally going to be featured here in Volume 0, but it ended up in Volume 5 instead, making the main story content of the volume relatively short. One of the big points of this volume was the appearance of Tama-san, the ayakashi who has "final boss"-level strength. Another thing featured here was a comprehensive breakdown of the twelve demon-slayer families that I put together as bonus material for the magazine serialization. It forced me to think about the background and data for every girl (ha!).

Table of Contents

"Hey! What do you guys think you're doing!?"

My name's Rinko Kuzaki, and I'm currently running full speed ahead to the elementary school grounds. It's them again. No matter how many times I teach those jerks a lesson, they just can't take a hint. There are three kids surrounding a little boy by the school gates. Even from this distance, I know just who they are. It's the bullies always tormenting that one little squirt when the teachers aren't looking.

"Oh great, it's Rinko. Here comes a real pest."

"Hmph! Today's the day we show her a thing or two! For just being a girl, she sure is a smartass."

That cheap excuse for a threat comes from the boys' chief in command, Gori.

Brand-new Novella
A TINY MEMORY FROM ONE DAY
WRITTEN BY: KOUGETSU MIKAZUKI
CANON/ILLUSTRATIONS: MILAN MATRA

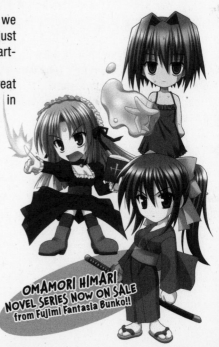

OMAMORI HIMARI
NOVEL SERIES NOW ON SALE
from Fujimi Fantasia Bunko!!

He's taller than me and built like a giant. Even though he's a third grader like me, anybody would think he's in at least sixth grade at first glance. It's guys like him who think they're so strong they can push anybody around. I see it all the time. And if you ask me, he's nothing but a big meathead!

"Picking on kids who are weaker than you is just pathetic! Today you'll suffer the wrath of Rinko-chan's Hyper-Ultra Miracle Fist of Justice!"

Like a real hero of justice, I jab an accusing finger at the three boys who were ganging up and beating on the one kid. Then I crouch down and aim a beautiful roundhouse kick to Gori's shin. Sure, my miniskirt flutters up in the wind, but you can't fight a decent fight if you're gonna worry about little details like that. First, you gotta take down the boss. So following typical battle protocol, I focus my efforts on defeating Gori.

"Hey! You said 'fist,' but that was a kick! That's not faaaaair!" Gori whines while tumbling to the ground. I glare down at him coldly and stick my tongue out.

"Hmph! It's called a figure of speech."

"Dammit, I won't forget this! Next time, you're goin' down! I'll make you regret you ever messed with me!"

That's the last thing Gori and his flunkies say before they run away with their tails between their legs.

My hands on my hips, I breathe a sigh of relief and then offer a hand to the boy crouched down in the dirt.

"......"

Ignoring my hand, he stands up and pats off the dirt from his clothes without a word. He's my neighbor, Yuuto Amakawa-kun. His body is black-and-blue from the daily beat downs he gets from those jerks. And it's like the teachers intentionally look the other way. Maybe they're afraid of Gori's dad. I just don't get how adults work sometimes. But letting bad things go on right in front of you is what cowards do. There's nothing more disgraceful than that. That's why I protect him. If you want something done, you gotta do it yourself.

"C'mon, you're coming home with me. My mom's making curry today, and I'm starved," I tell him cheerfully, pretending nothing's happened.

But he's as silent as ever. Not even a hint of a smile. He always has that deadpan face on, showing no sign of emotion. I find something unsettling about that poker face of his. Maybe that's why he gets picked on so bad. But he's been like that since I first met him. From the very beginning, I never liked the way his eyes always looked so lifeless. I've tried to make him smile by having him read funny comics and watch comedy shows. I've tried everything under the sun, but to no avail. It's just hard to believe that after all my painstaking efforts, he won't so much as crack a smile.

And I've had just about enough. I'm gonna have to resort to force.

"...Take that!"

I shove my fingers into the corners of his mouth and pull up. Yuuto only blinks at me in surprise.

"C'mon, it's called a smile. Try it for once," I say, pursing my lips as I glance at him.

But just as I expected, all he does is drop his head. Not that I really had all that high a hope for a response.

"I know you probably don't feel like smiling. But if you try it, even if it's just for fun, you might get a kick outta it and start smiling for real... I just thought you might like that."

Suddenly realizing that I could be bothering him or making him mad, a wave of anxiety sweeps over my heart.

"......"

Just as I thought. No response.

Why does he have to be so quiet? This conversation's not going anywhere. Feeling embarrassed, I pull my fingers out of his mouth and make my way to the gates to start my walk home. But it's tough to just go home and leave him all alone like that. I should knock some sense into myself and quit meddling in his business. Why do I even bother as much as I do? Is it 'cos I've never come across somebody quite like Yuuto-kun before? Or is it something else?

Shaking my head at the mere thought, I can't help glancing back at him. Yuuto-kun's blank look hasn't changed, but now he's following me.

Once I realize that, I slow my pace so that Yuuto-kun can quickly trot up to me. It's nothing big, but I feel my chest suddenly grow warm. It's the strangest thing... It's like all that awkwardness I was feeling a minute ago never was. Without a word between us, we take to the street as the setting sun bathes it in gold. Not having words or facial expressions to rely on can be a little unsettling at first, but after looking at Yuuto-kun more closely, I feel like I've gotten a better handle on just what's going through his head. I don't even mind how tight-lipped he is. It doesn't mean that he doesn't feel anything. Maybe it's just he's not very good at interacting with people? Maybe he just can't express his feelings well.

The next day...

I'm walking home with Yuuto as usual when I stop in my tracks. Ahead of me, I see Gori. Only today it's not just Gori. A kid almost twice Gori's size is standing before us with his feet planted firmly apart.

"Hmph. I warned you I'd be back to settle the score. Big bro, that's her. The cheeky little bitch. Avenge your kid brother and teach her a lesson."

"Dude, you seriously lost to a puny squirt like her? How lame! Don't embarrass your brother like that."

"B-b-but she plays dirty!"

"Plays dirty!? I was just using my head, okay? Don't you know the brain's your biggest weapon? Got a problem with that?"

I'm not about to let some scum say I don't play fair. The moment the words leave my mouth, I know I'm in for it now. Gori's brother twists his face into a frown and cracks his massive knuckles.

"Well, well. Aren't you the big talker? I hate a girl who doesn't know her place. Maybe a good smack or two'll teach you some humility? I'm sure you're way cuter when you can't open your mouth."

"......!?"

All it would've taken to keep these goons away was not pissing them off. And I just went and pissed them off. In short, I pretty much picked this fight. Usually, I'd be more than happy to walk into a scrap somebody's picked with me. But there're also times when you should just walk away.

Slowly, Gori's big brother lumbers toward us with his massive form. I hold my breath and brace myself, my eyes scanning the area for any immediate route of escape. That's when Yuuto-kun takes a step forward and shields me with his body.

"Huh? Y-Yuuto-kun?"

"......"

I'm always the one protecting him, and he's always the one who never does a thing and accepts it indifferently.

Now he's suddenly trying to protect me? I can hardly believe what's happening before my very eyes.

"D-don't do it. They're too strong for you...," I say as I grab his hand and try to pull him back.

But he shakes free of my grasp and fixes his gaze straight ahead. The expression I can glean from his profile is as vague as ever, but he does seem awfully manly all of a sudden. It sets my heart thumping loud and strong. I'm sorry, but no matter how hard Yuuto-kun may try, there's no way he can win against a bully as big as this kid, especially if his little brother doesn't even break a sweat pummeling Yuuto-kun the way he always does.

"Run away! I'm telling you, it's no use!" I plead with him, but he only shakes his head slowly.

"You little twerp! Don't go tryin' to act like a big man just 'cos there's a girl watching!"

The older brother's fist makes brutal contact with the side of Yuuto-kun's face, sending him flying into the wall, where he crumples to the ground.

"Stop it! That's enough! You came to settle the score with me, remember!?" I yell, launching a kick at the older boy's groin. But before I can touch him, he parries my move.

"Hits below the belt are against the rules. Didn'cha know that?" he says with a smirk as he catches the ankle of my kicking leg and yanks me toward him.

"!?"

I find myself with my legs spread wide like a ballerina. And my ankle's aching. My skirt's totally hiked up, exposing my legs and panties to the world.

"St-stop it... Kn-knock it off right now!"

"Aaw, strawberry print. You really are just a little baby."

"Stop..."

Gori's big brother ogles my underwear with a dirty look in his eyes. I've never cared about my skirt fluttering up every now and then, but I can't stand the way his eyes seem glued to me.

"I told you to knock it off this instant..."

"If you use your manners and ask me nice, I'll let your leg down," he says in an aroused way, breathing in heavy snorts through his nose.

"...Kuh! Not on your life! Scum like you don't deserve manners."

"Fine then. I'll just have to give you a little punishment."

With that, the older brother starts to reach his other hand toward my panties.

"Wh-what do you think you're doing!?"

"How about we play doctor, hm?"

"Wow, big bro, I shoulda known you'd take things all the way!"

The two brothers laugh obscenely and start to tug at my underwear.

This can't be happening. They're joking, right? Anybody could pass by at any moment here! I start to panic as things take an unexpected turn. That's when...Yuuto-kun's back on his feet before I even realize it, and he's clamping down on the older brother's wrist with his jaws.

"Gyaaaaaahn! O-ooooooow! You little shit!!"

The hand that was trying to yank down my underwear suddenly nails Yuuto-kun in the face. But Yuuto-kun's teeth hold fast, and he doesn't stop biting down on the older brother's wrist.

"L-listen, you! Stop that! I told you to stop that right now!"

Gori lands a kick right in Yuuto-kun's stomach. But still Yuuto-kun's mouth remains fixed on him, no signs of letting go.

"H-he's crazy... This seriously hurts! Ow! Ow! Owwww! My hand! Gimme back my hand!!"

Gori's brother is screaming now and savagely pummels the side of Yuuto-kun's face over and over. In no time at all, his face is a swollen mass of purple.

"Yuuto-kun! Stop it! That's enough! You don't have to do this!" I scream at him, but as usual, my words pass right through.

He doesn't let go. Just when I'm thinking Yuuto-kun won't last much longer, a saving voice rings out.

"Hey, you! What're you doing over there!?"

The moment the teacher's voice is heard, Gori's older brother lets go of my leg and runs for it, full speed.

Gori's right behind him, the teacher coming up fast.

Left alone, Yuuto-kun and I collapse to the ground on our knees, our shoulders heaving up and down. Now's when the shakes set in, and I'm shocked at this unexpected reaction.

"That's funny, what's going on...? I should be fine, so what is this?"

It must be some kind of wave of relief that sends my nose stinging and my eyes glazing over. I quickly look to the sky but already my eyes are wet, and my vision's swimming.

"Rinko-chan. Are you okay?"

"Y-yeah... Of course, I'm fine!"

It feels like a long time since I last heard Yuuto-kun's voice. I'm surprised but too busy trying to avoid his eyes until my tears have adequately dried. I don't want anybody to see me crying. It'd be too pathetic. Finally, my vision clears, and I turn to look at Yuuto-kun. I finding him staring deep into my eyes searchingly.

"I said I'm fine. What about you, Yuuto-kun? Your face looks pretty puffed up," I say, looking away.

He only nods in agreement. When all's said and done, Yuuto-kun's got a pretty cute face, and I can't bear seeing it ballooned with painful splotches of red and purple like this.

"...I'm sorry. It's 'cos of me that you got so hurt."

He only shakes his head at my words.

"I mean it, I shouldn't have provoked him like that. I'm really sorry."

Having to admit to myself that I was the cause of all Yuuto-kun's pain is so infuriating, I'm quickly filled with regret. I let my shoulders sink and stare at the ground. Yuuto-kun unexpectedly lays a hand on my shoulder. I'm so surprised by the gesture that I lift my face, only to find him sticking his fingers in the corners of my mouth and pulling up on them the way I did to him before. Just being forced to smile lifts my spirits some. I try to smile, and he nods, looking satisfied.

"Aha, that's right. There's something else I should be saying after what happened... Thank you."

The moment I utter those words, Yuuto-kun's eyes open wide, and his face flushes. It's just a twitch, but I could swear that the corners of his mouth lifted the tiniest bit. I've never seen Yuuto-kun make that kind of face before. It's the faintest smile, and you'd never be able to tell what it was at first glance, but after all my efforts in trying to make him smile, I'm sure of it.

"...Well, well. So you really can smile."

"Huh?"

"You oughta keep it up."

"You think so? I'm not so sure, though...," Yuuto says shyly, scratching his head.

It's odd. All the times I've protected him from those bullies, he never once smiled.

"Now I get it... I shouldn't have tried protecting you. Guys don't like that... That explains it."

"...I'm going to grow strong enough to protect you, Rinko-chan."

Upon hearing those words, my whole body suddenly suffuses with heat. What's this strange feeling? I don't think I've ever felt anything like it. I'm suddenly short of breath, and my head feels light. But all I can say is the typical stuff.

"Yeah, but I'm stronger than you! You'll have to work wicked hard if you wanna protect me, got it?"

"I know. I will," Yuuto-kun replies, picking up his purple charm off the ground and gazing at it.

Then he mutters under his breath, "I'd much rather protect people than be protected."

His profile looks so sad and lonely that I pull his head into an embrace without a second thought.

***

It appears that after eating dinner and cleaning up, I caught a few z's. But that won't do! If you fall asleep right after eating, you'll find yourself heading straight for fatso-ville. I rub my eyes and lift my head off the kitchen table. I guess I fell asleep flat on my face without realizing it.

"I had that dream again..."

The one about the first time Yuuto showed me an expression. A smile, no less.

From time to time, I still have dreams about that day. I wonder if Yuuto even remembers it himself. It's already been seven years since then. After that day, I stopped protecting him. I'd thought that he just didn't know how to interact with people, and that's why I was trying to change him. And before I knew it, he had changed. He started warming up to those around him and even making friends and smiling.

"...Maybe he changed too much."

I narrow my eyes and lock them on the sofa in the living room.

"Young Lord, I tell you time and again that sharing a bed with her master is a servant's duty. Now, allow me to spend the night with you."

"...I would do a much better job at putting Yuuto in a dreamy state of mind than some cat...you know."

Himari has her hands around Yuuto's neck from behind, pressing his head into her oversized boobs, while Shizuku's doing what she always does, stroking his thighs and quietly sneaking her hands to more private areas. Hold it! That's enough!!

"You gotta be more on your guard! Whaddaya think you're doing, letting them confuse you!!?" I yell at the top of my lungs, grabbing my trusty "Rinko-chan's Violent Love Part II" nail bat.

Yuuto may protect me now, but I've been reduced to just protecting his chastity... Himari harbors all sorts of evils in those giant melons of hers. And let's not forget Lizlet.

Shizuku's trying to take Yuuto down a dark path by using her Lolita-ness as a weapon, and Kuesu was betrothed to him by their parents. Yuuto is currently surrounded by cute girls on all sides. And if given a chance, they'd gladly try to nail him. So though I've been called a flat-chested commoner, I'm so not about to lose to them. I'm probably the only one who can protect the "natural everyday life" Yuuto dreams of—

THE END

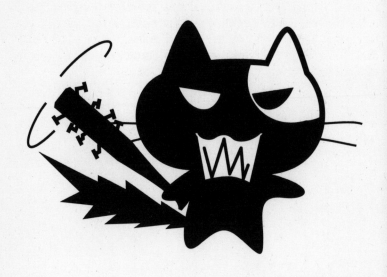

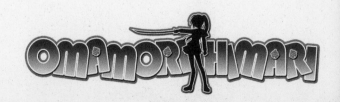

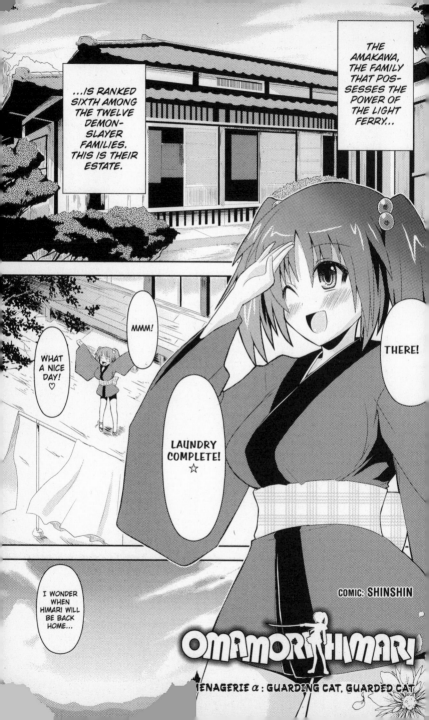

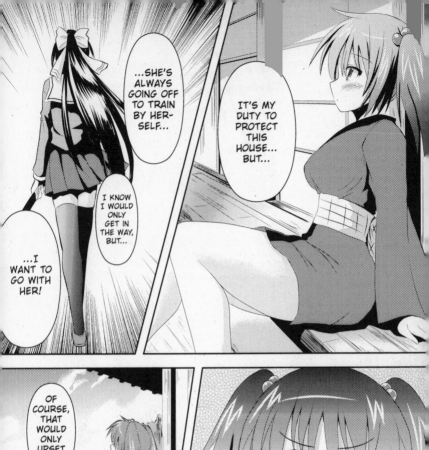

...SHE'S ALWAYS GOING OFF TO TRAIN BY HER-SELF...

IT'S MY DUTY TO PROTECT THIS HOUSE... BUT...

I KNOW I WOULD ONLY GET IN THE WAY, BUT...

...I WANT TO GO WITH HER!

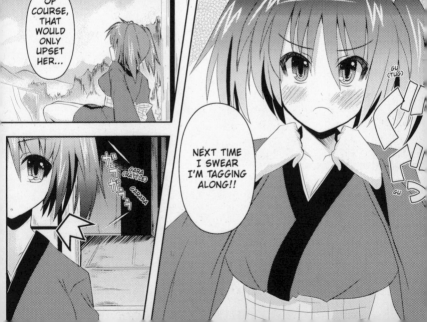

OF COURSE, THAT WOULD ONLY UPSET HER...

GU (TUG)

GU

NEXT TIME I SWEAR I'M TAGGING ALONG!!

SARA (RATTLE)

GARARA

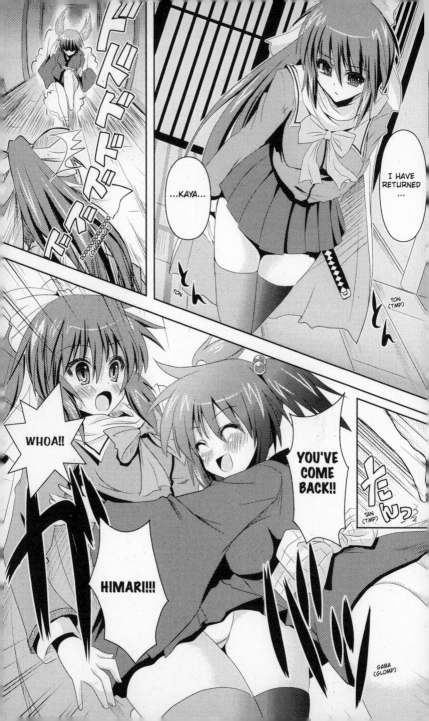

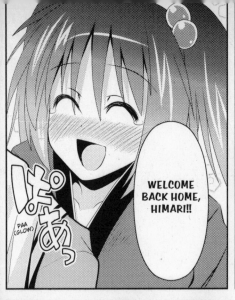

WELCOME BACK HOME, HIMARI!!

PAA (GLOW)

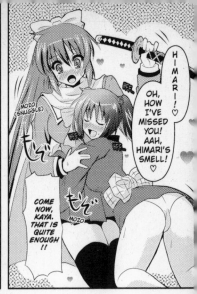

HIMARI!♡

OH, HOW I'VE MISSED YOU! AAH, HIMARI'S SMELL!

COME NOW, KAYA. THAT IS QUITE ENOUGH!!

MOZO (SNUGGLE)

MOZO

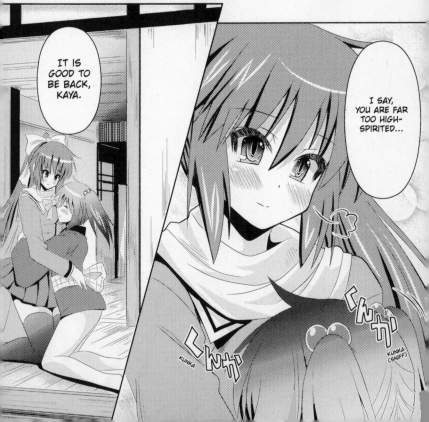

IT IS GOOD TO BE BACK, KAYA.

I SAY, YOU ARE FAR TOO HIGH-SPIRITED...

KUNKA

KUNKA (SNIFF)

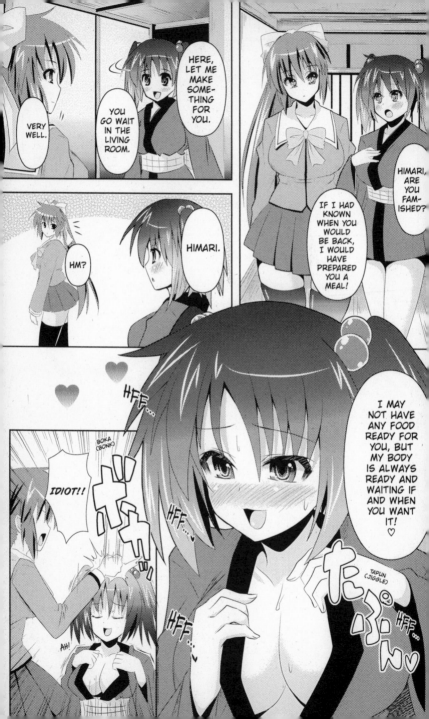

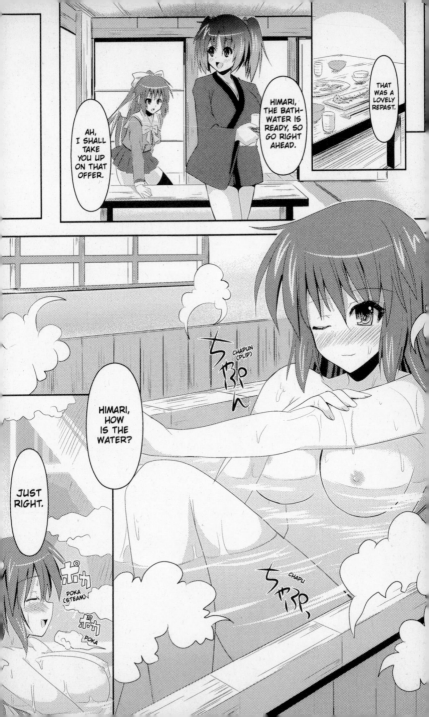

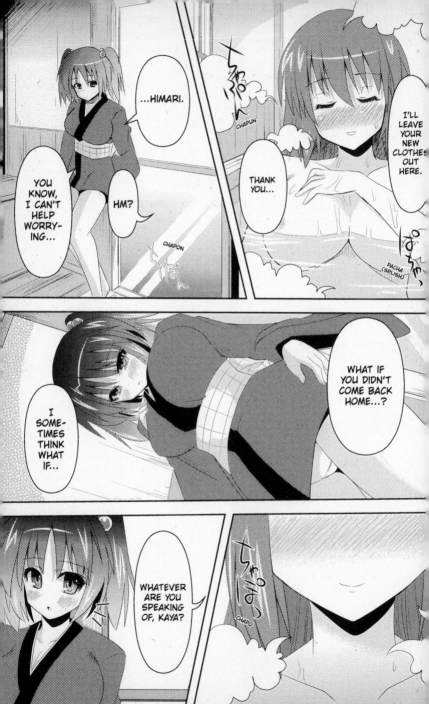

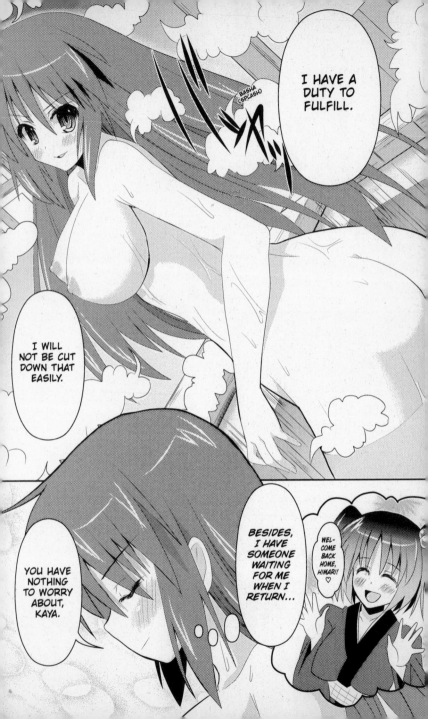

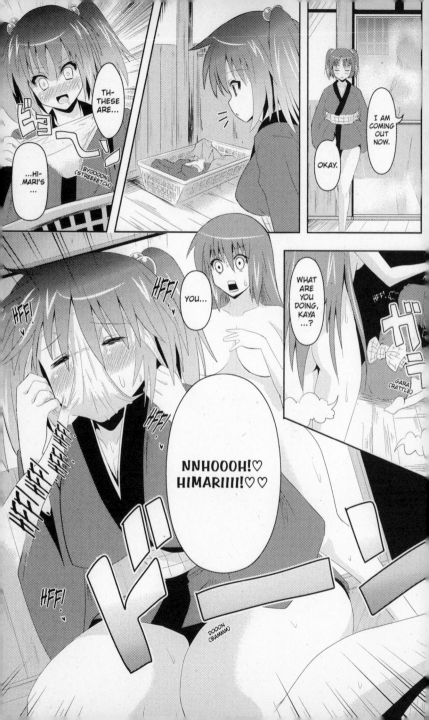

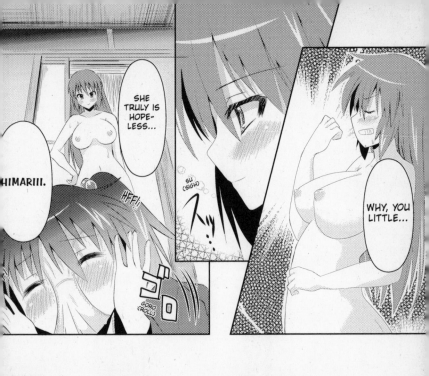

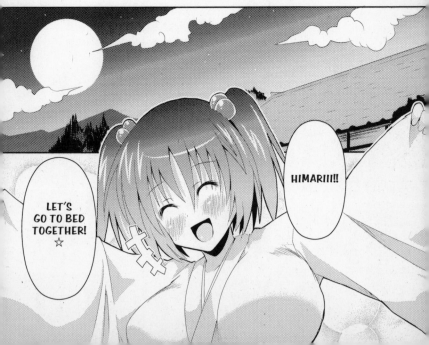

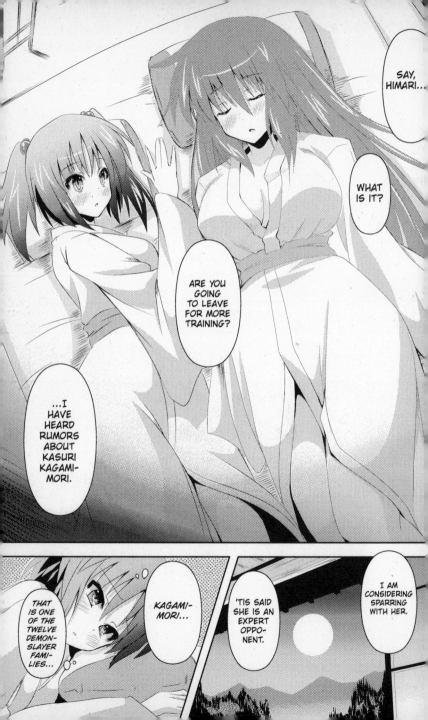

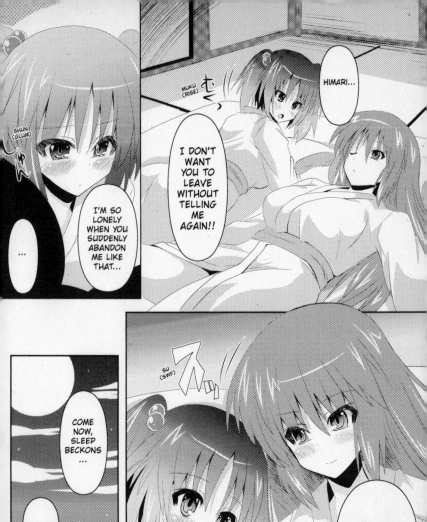

HIMARI...

MUKU
(RISE)

I DON'T WANT YOU TO LEAVE WITHOUT TELLING ME AGAIN!!

SHUN
(GLUM)

I'M SO LONELY WHEN YOU SUDDENLY ABANDON ME LIKE THAT...

...

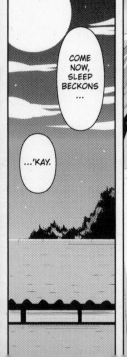

COME NOW, SLEEP BECKONS ...

...'KAY.

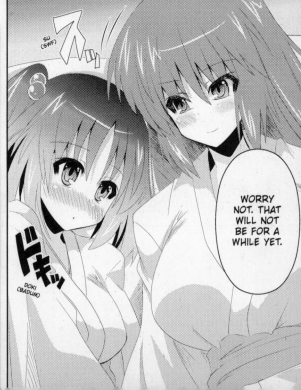

SU
(SWF)

WORRY NOT. THAT WILL NOT BE FOR A WHILE YET.

DOKI
(BADUM)

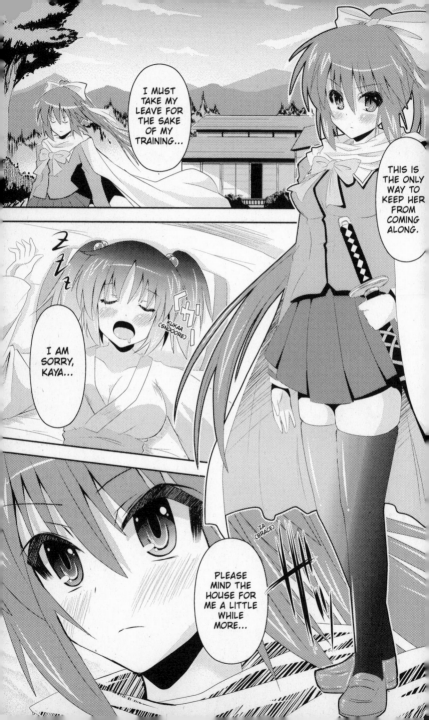

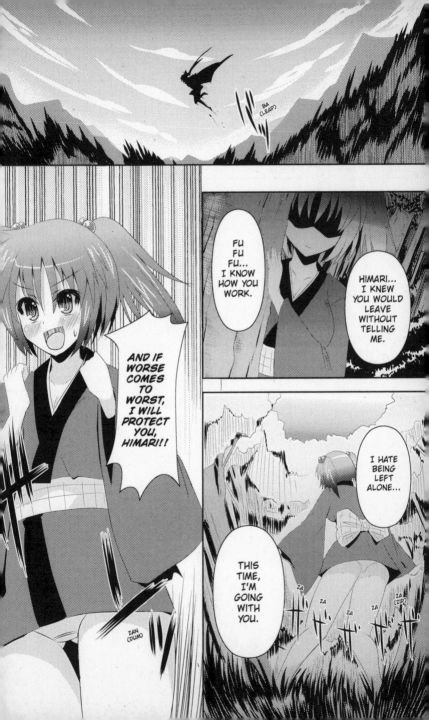

BA
(LEAP)

FU
FU
FU...
I KNOW
HOW YOU
WORK.

HIMARI...
I KNEW
YOU WOULD
LEAVE
WITHOUT
TELLING
ME.

AND IF
WORSE
COMES
TO
WORST,
I WILL
PROTECT
YOU,
HIMARI!!

I HATE
BEING
LEFT
ALONE...

THIS
TIME,
I'M
GOING
WITH
YOU.

ZA

ZA

ZA

ZA

ZA
(ZIP)

ZAN
(DUN)

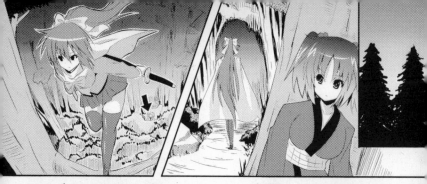
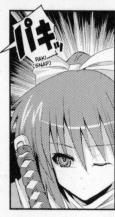
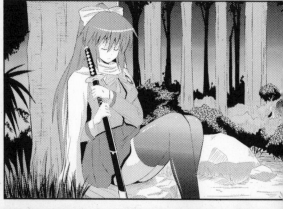
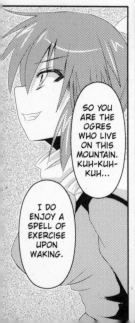
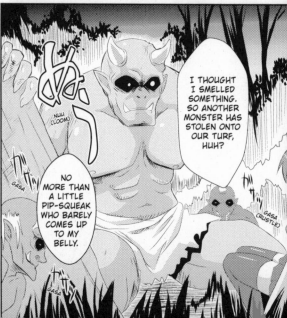

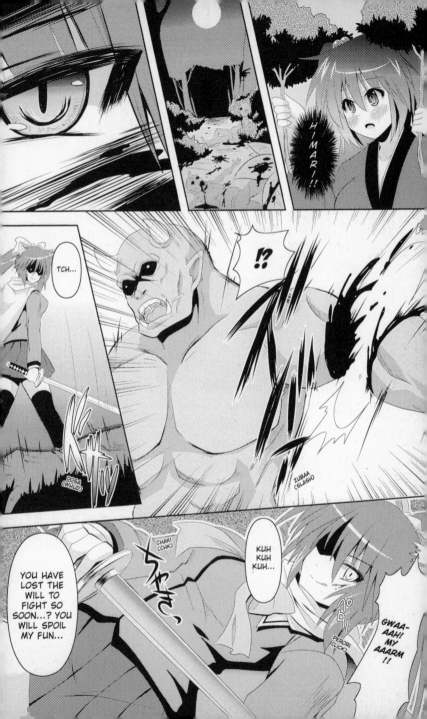

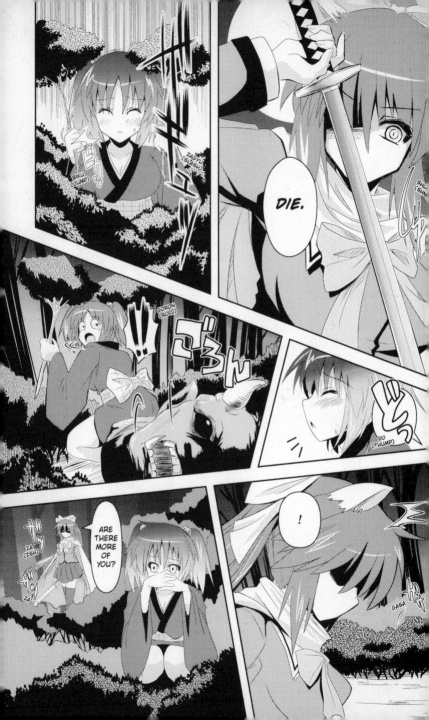

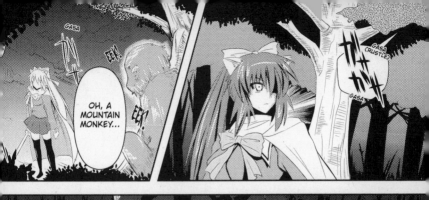

OH, A
MOUNTAIN
MONKEY...

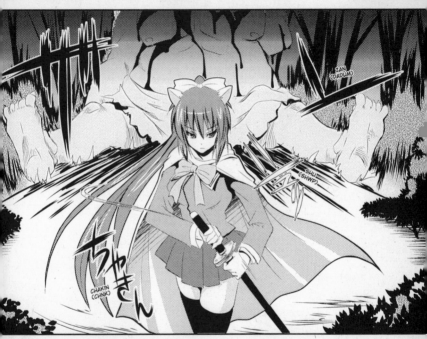

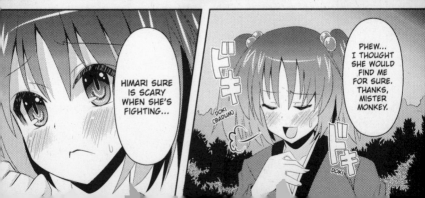

HIMARI SURE
IS SCARY
WHEN SHE'S
FIGHTING...

PHEW...
I THOUGHT
SHE WOULD
FIND ME
FOR SURE.
THANKS,
MISTER
MONKEY.

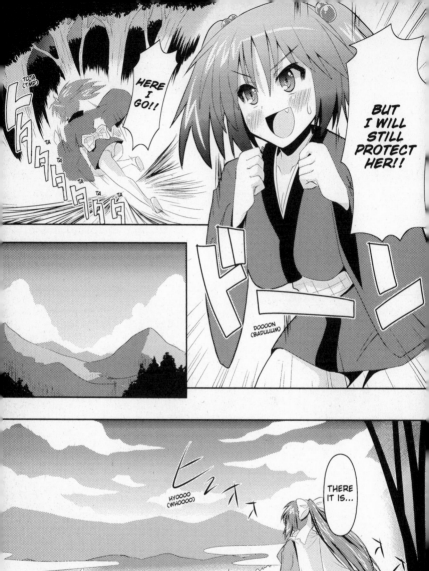

HERE
I GO!!

BUT
I WILL
STILL
PROTECT
HER!!

TOTA
(TAP)

TA
TA
TA
TA

DOOON
(BADUUUM)

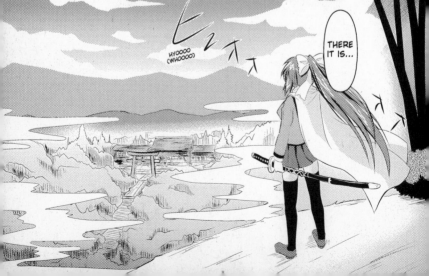

HYOOOO
(WHOOOO)

THERE
IT IS...

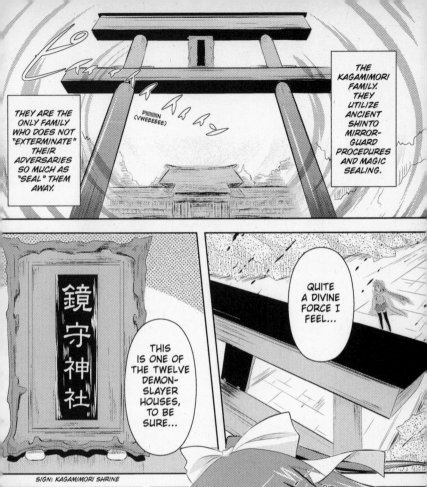

THE KAGAMIMORI FAMILY. THEY UTILIZE ANCIENT SHINTO MIRROR-GUARD PROCEDURES AND MAGIC SEALING.

THEY ARE THE ONLY FAMILY WHO DOES NOT "EXTERMINATE" THEIR ADVERSARIES SO MUCH AS "SEAL" THEM AWAY.

PIIIIIIIIN
(VWEEEEEE)

鏡守神社

THIS IS ONE OF THE TWELVE DEMON-SLAYER HOUSES, TO BE SURE...

QUITE A DIVINE FORCE I FEEL...

SIGN: KAGAMIMORI SHRINE

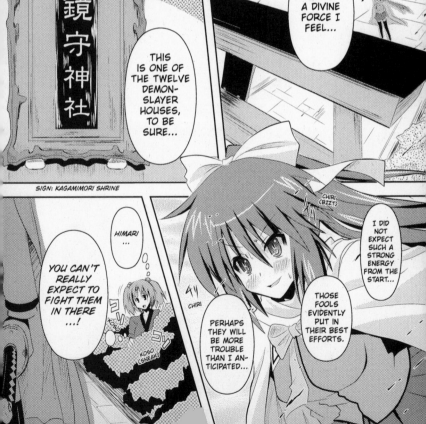

HIMARI...

YOU CAN'T REALLY EXPECT TO FIGHT THEM IN THERE...!

KOSO
(SNEAKS)

PERHAPS THEY WILL BE MORE TROUBLE THAN I ANTICIPATED...

CHIRI
(BZZT)

CHIRI

I DID NOT EXPECT SUCH A STRONG ENERGY FROM THE START...

THOSE FOOLS EVIDENTLY PUT IN THEIR BEST EFFORTS.

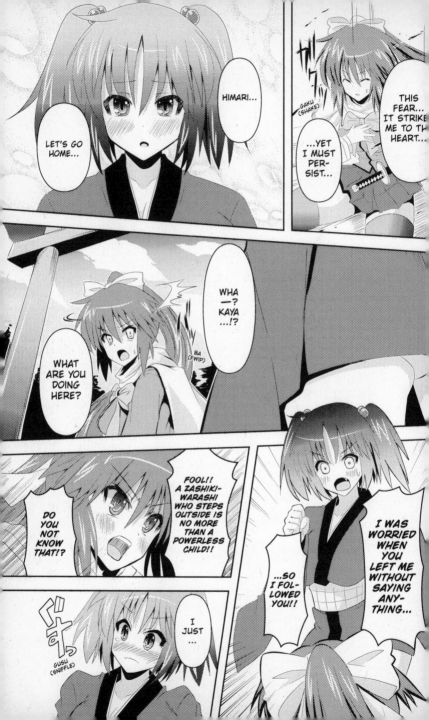

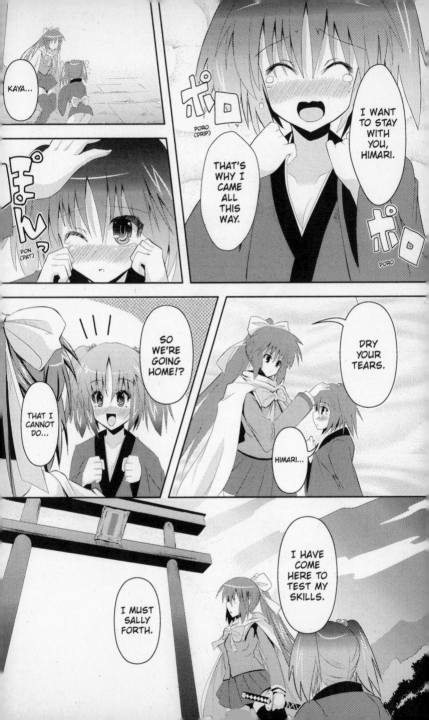

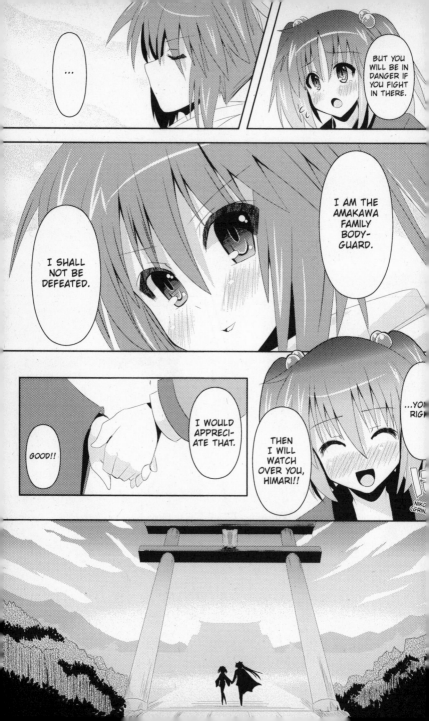

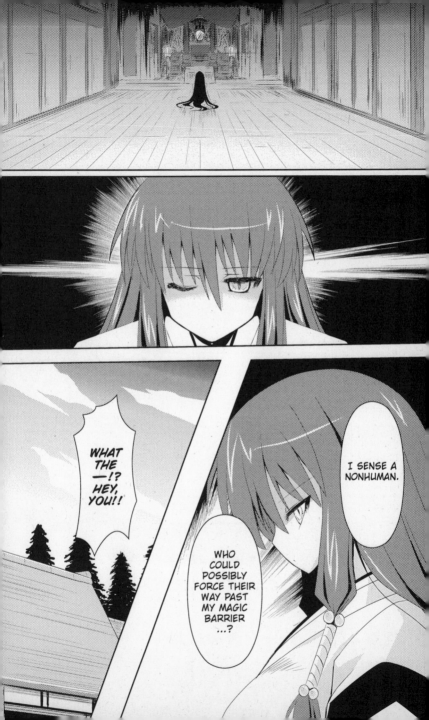

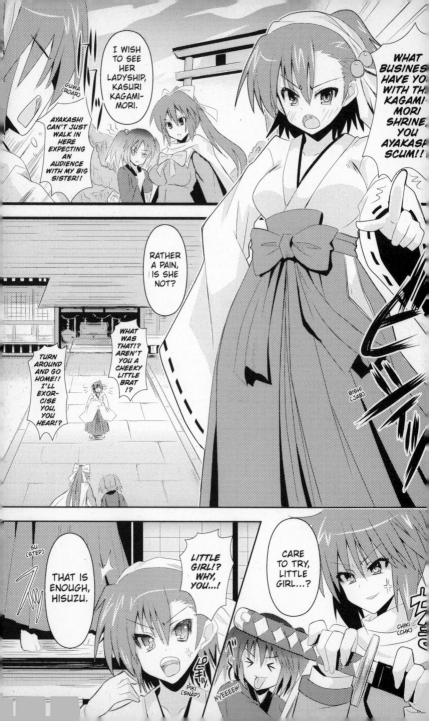

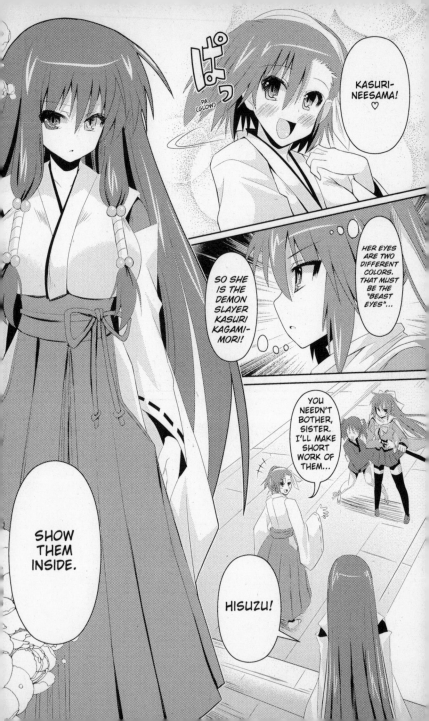

KASURI-NEESAMA! ♥

PA (GLOW)

HER EYES ARE TWO DIFFERENT COLORS. THAT MUST BE THE "BEAST EYES"...

SO SHE IS THE DEMON SLAYER KASURI KAGAMI-MORI!!

YOU NEEDN'T BOTHER, SISTER. I'LL MAKE SHORT WORK OF THEM...

SHOW THEM INSIDE.

HISUZU!

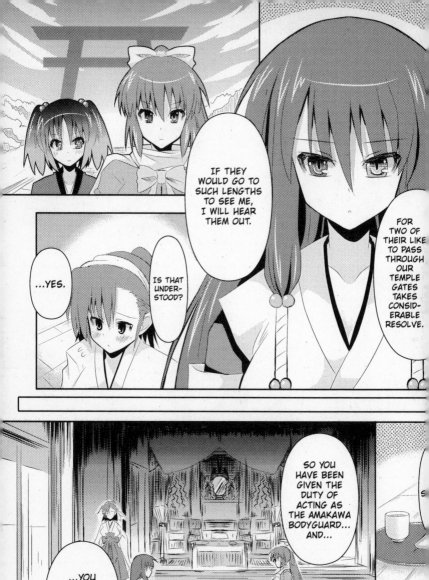

IF THEY WOULD GO TO SUCH LENGTHS TO SEE ME, I WILL HEAR THEM OUT.

FOR TWO OF THEIR LIKE TO PASS THROUGH OUR TEMPLE GATES TAKES CONSIDERABLE RESOLVE.

...YES.

IS THAT UNDERSTOOD?

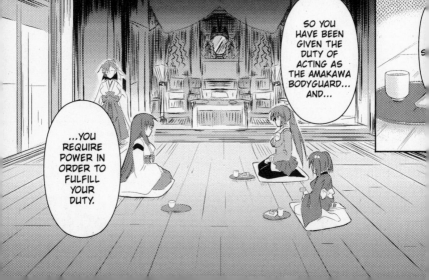

SO YOU HAVE BEEN GIVEN THE DUTY OF ACTING AS THE AMAKAWA BODYGUARD... AND...

...YOU REQUIRE POWER IN ORDER TO FULFILL YOUR DUTY.

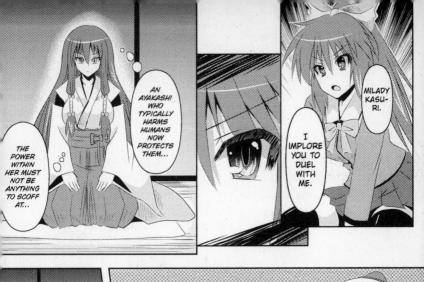

AN AYAKASHI WHO TYPICALLY HARMS HUMANS NOW PROTECTS THEM...

THE POWER WITHIN HER MUST NOT BE ANYTHING TO SCOFF AT...

MILADY KASURI.

I IMPLORE YOU TO DUEL WITH ME.

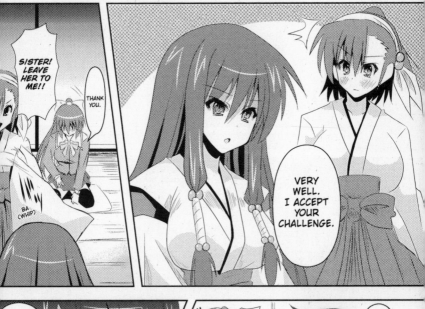

SISTER! LEAVE HER TO ME!!

THANK YOU.

BA (WHIP)

VERY WELL. I ACCEPT YOUR CHALLENGE.

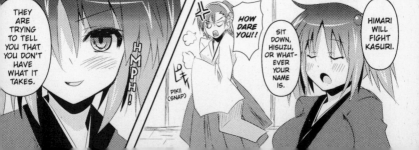

THEY ARE TRYING TO TELL YOU THAT YOU DON'T HAVE WHAT IT TAKES.

HMPH!

HOW DARE YOU!!

PIKI! (SNAP)

SIT DOWN, HISUZU, OR WHAT-EVER YOUR NAME IS.

HIMARI WILL FIGHT KASURI.

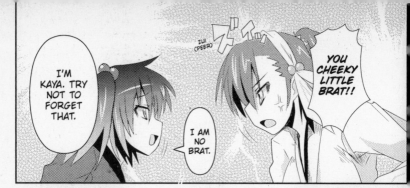

I'M KAYA. TRY NOT TO FORGET THAT.

I AM NO BRAT.

ZUI (PEER)

YOU CHEEKY LITTLE BRAT!!

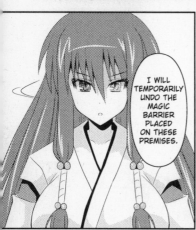

I WILL TEMPORARILY UNDO THE MAGIC BARRIER PLACED ON THESE PREMISES.

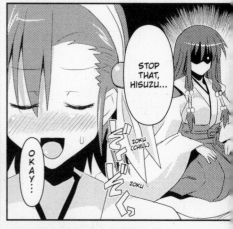

STOP THAT, HISUZU...

OKAY...

ZOKU (CHILL)

ZOKU

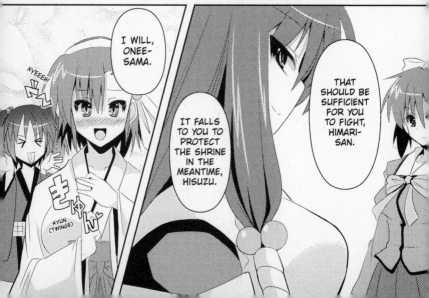

I WILL, ONEE-SAMA.

NYEEEH!

KYUN (TWINGE)

IT FALLS TO YOU TO PROTECT THE SHRINE IN THE MEANTIME, HISUZU.

THAT SHOULD BE SUFFICIENT FOR YOU TO FIGHT, HIMARI-SAN.

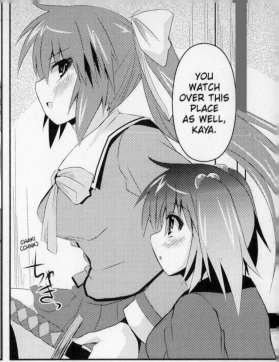

YOU WATCH OVER THIS PLACE AS WELL, KAYA.

CHAKI (CHNK)

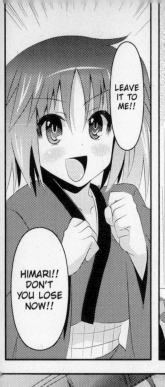

LEAVE IT TO ME!!

HIMARI!! DON'T YOU LOSE NOW!!

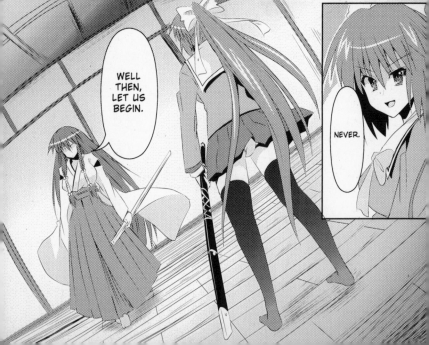

WELL THEN, LET US BEGIN.

NEVER.

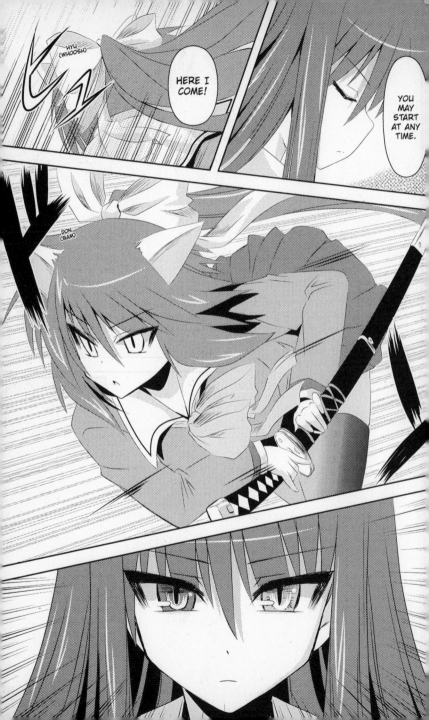

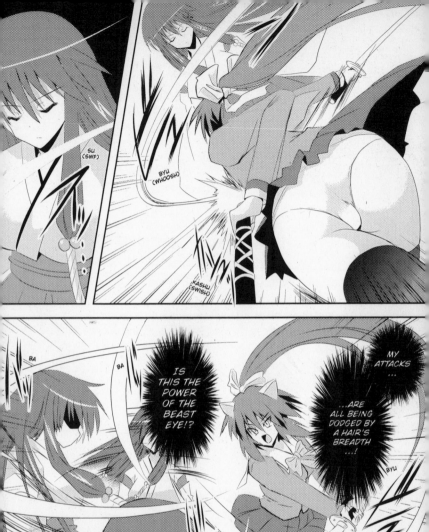

SU
(SWF)

BYU
(WHOOSH)

KASHU
(SWISH)

BA

BA

IS THIS THE POWER OF THE BEAST EYE!?

MY ATTACKS...

...ARE ALL BEING DODGED BY A HAIR'S BREADTH...!

BYU

BA

BA
(DODGE)

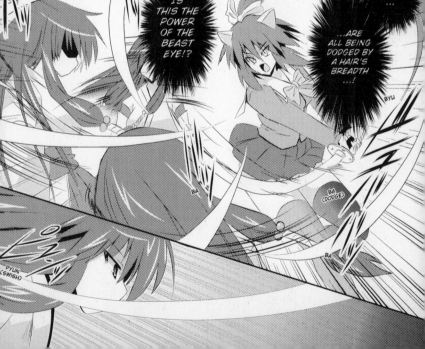

PYUN
(SWISH)

BA

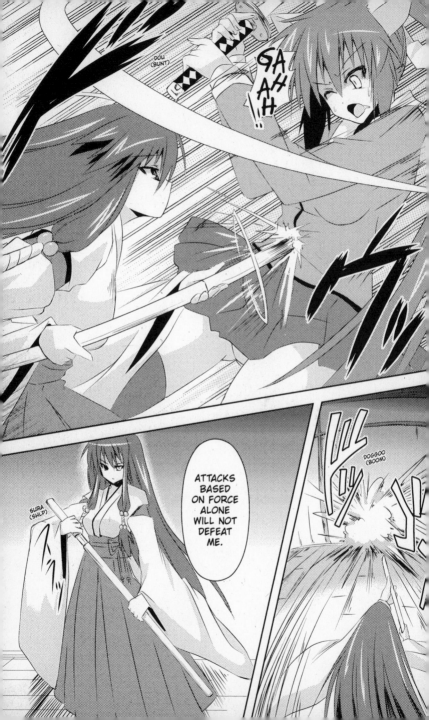

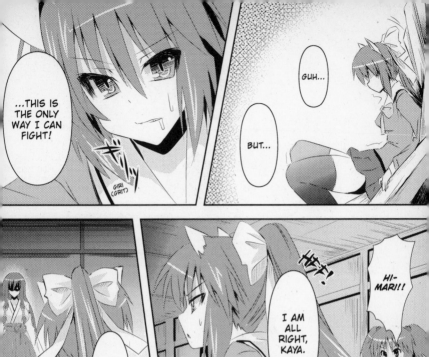

...THIS IS THE ONLY WAY I CAN FIGHT!

GIRI (GRIT)

GUH...

BUT...

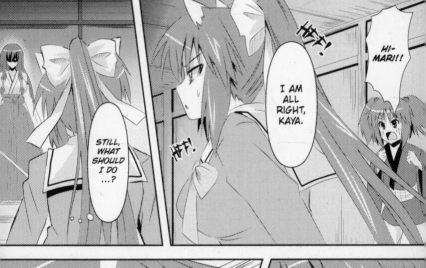

STILL, WHAT SHOULD I DO...?

I AM ALL RIGHT, KAYA.

‼

HI-MARI!!

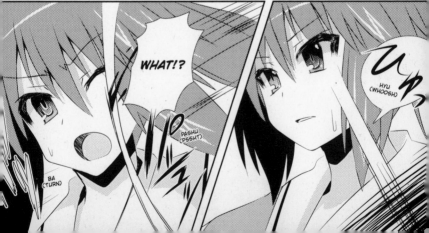

WHAT!?

PASHU (PSSHT)

HYU (WHOOSH)

BA (TURN)

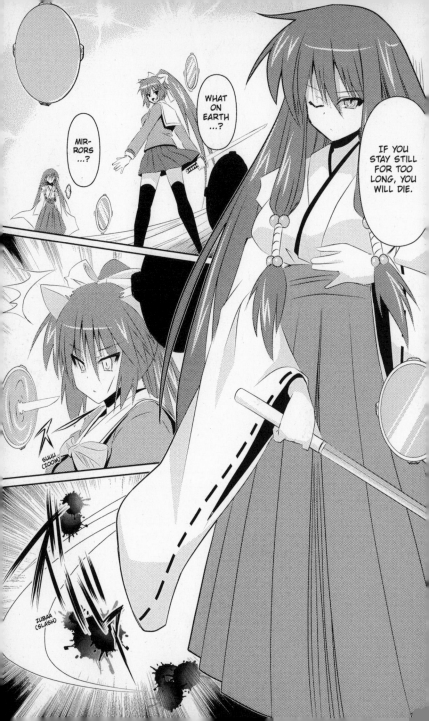

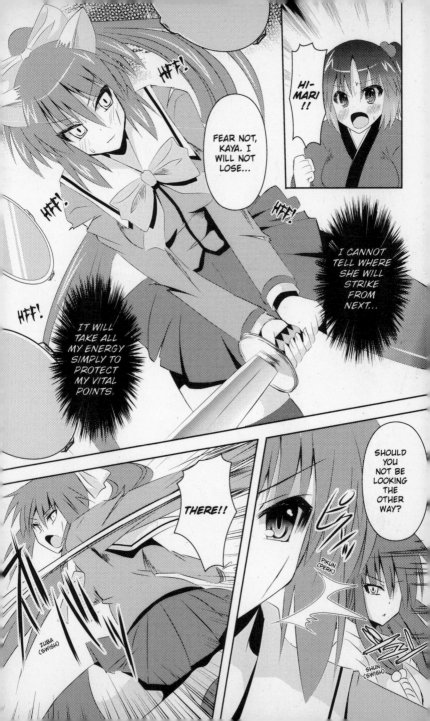

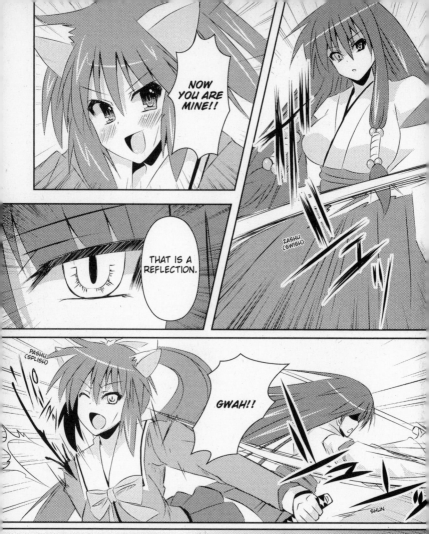

NOW YOU ARE MINE!!

THAT IS A REFLECTION.

ZASHU
(SWISH)

PASHU
(SPLISH)

GWAH!!

SHUN

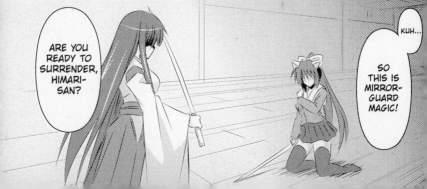

ARE YOU READY TO SURRENDER, HIMARI-SAN?

KUH...

SO THIS IS MIRROR-GUARD MAGIC!

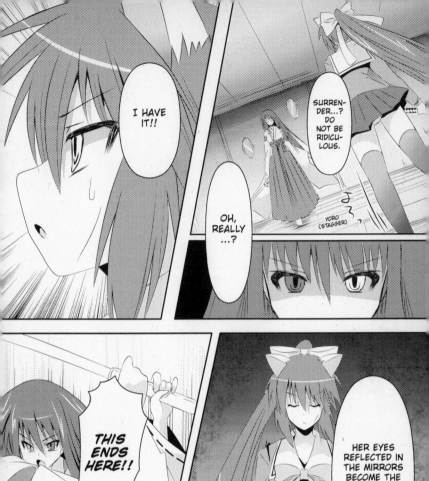

I HAVE IT!!

SURRENDER...? DO NOT BE RIDICULOUS.

OH, REALLY...?

YORO
(STAGGER)

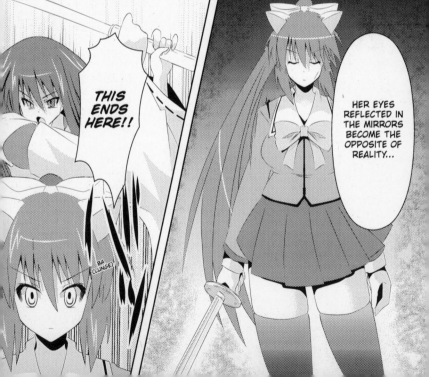

THIS ENDS HERE!!

BA
(LUNGE)

HER EYES REFLECTED IN THE MIRRORS BECOME THE OPPOSITE OF REALITY...

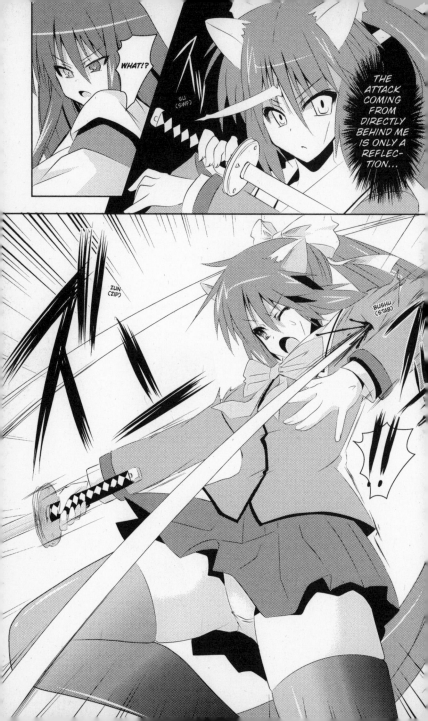

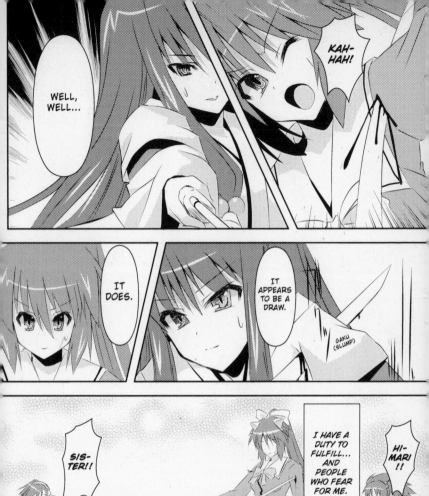

WELL, WELL...

KAH-HAH!

IT DOES.

IT APPEARS TO BE A DRAW.

GAKU
(SLUMP)

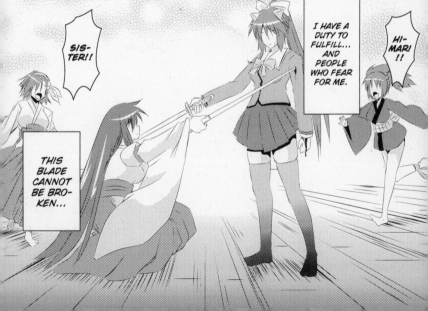

SIS-TER!!

I HAVE A DUTY TO FULFILL... AND PEOPLE WHO FEAR FOR ME.

HI-MARI!!

THIS BLADE CANNOT BE BRO-KEN...

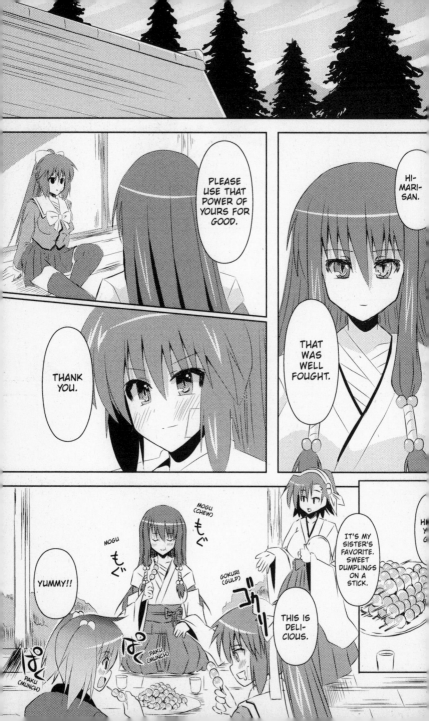

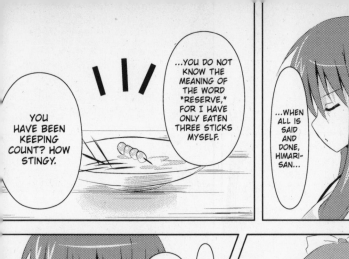

...YOU DO NOT KNOW THE MEANING OF THE WORD "RESERVE," FOR I HAVE ONLY EATEN THREE STICKS MYSELF.

YOU HAVE BEEN KEEPING COUNT? HOW STINGY.

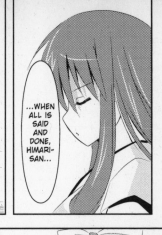

...WHEN ALL IS SAID AND DONE, HIMARI-SAN...

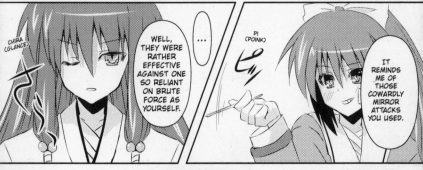

CHIRA (GLANCE)

WELL, THEY WERE RATHER EFFECTIVE AGAINST ONE SO RELIANT ON BRUTE FORCE AS YOURSELF.

...

PI (POINK)

IT REMINDS ME OF THOSE COWARDLY MIRROR ATTACKS YOU USED.

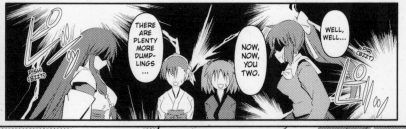

PISHI (BZZT)

THERE ARE PLENTY MORE DUMPLINGS...

NOW, NOW, YOU TWO.

WELL, WELL...

PIRI (BZZT)

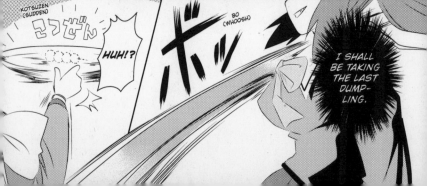

KOTSUZEN (SUDDEN)

こうぜん

HUH!?

ボ

BO (WHOOSH)

I SHALL BE TAKING THE LAST DUMPLING.

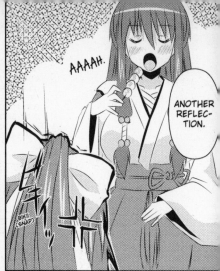

AAAAH.

ANOTHER REFLECTION.

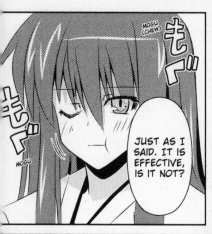

MOGU (CHEW)

JUST AS I SAID. IT IS EFFECTIVE, IS IT NOT?

MOGU

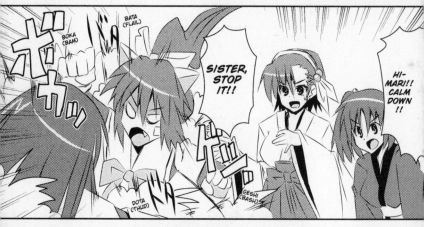

BATA (FLAIL)

BOKA (BAM)

SISTER, STOP IT!!

HI-MARI!! CALM DOWN!!

DOTA (THUD)

GESHI (BASH)

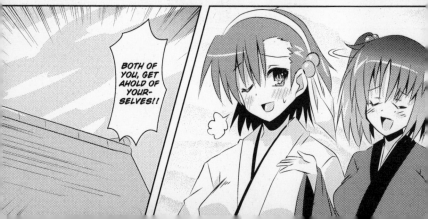

BOTH OF YOU, GET AHOLD OF YOUR-SELVES!!

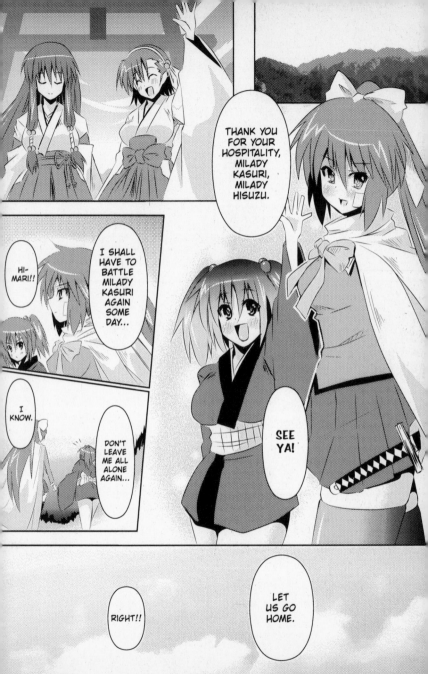

THANK YOU FOR YOUR HOSPITALITY, MILADY KASURI, MILADY HISUZU.

HI-MARI!!

I SHALL HAVE TO BATTLE MILADY KASURI AGAIN SOME DAY...

I KNOW.

DON'T LEAVE ME ALL ALONE AGAIN...

SEE YA!

RIGHT!!

LET US GO HOME.

THE END

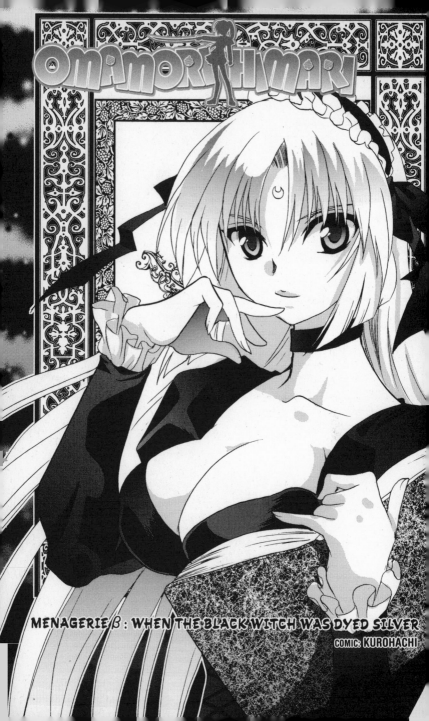

MENAGERIE β : WHEN THE BLACK WITCH WAS DYED SILVER

COMIC: KUROHACHI

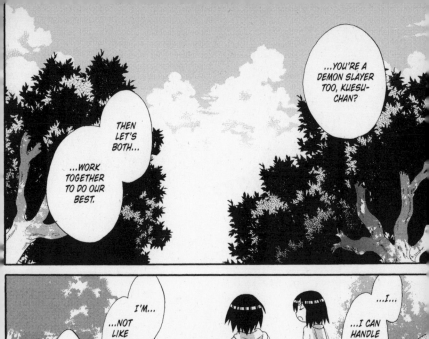

...YOU'RE A DEMON SLAYER TOO, KUESU-CHAN?

THEN LET'S BOTH...

...WORK TOGETHER TO DO OUR BEST.

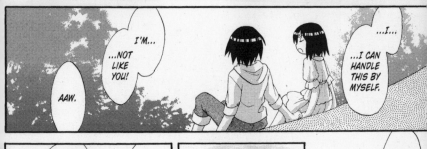

I'M...

...NOT LIKE YOU!

AAW.

...I...

...I CAN HANDLE THIS BY MYSELF.

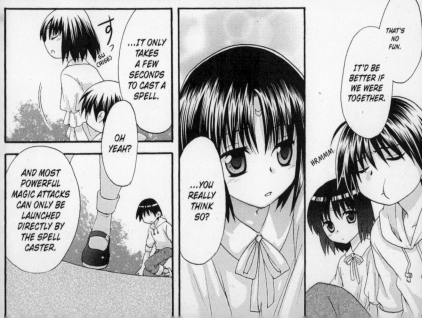

す
SU
(RISE)

...IT ONLY TAKES A FEW SECONDS TO CAST A SPELL.

OH YEAH?

AND MOST POWERFUL MAGIC ATTACKS CAN ONLY BE LAUNCHED DIRECTLY BY THE SPELL CASTER.

....YOU REALLY THINK SO?

THAT'S NO FUN.

IT'D BE BETTER IF WE WERE TOGETHER.

HRMMM.

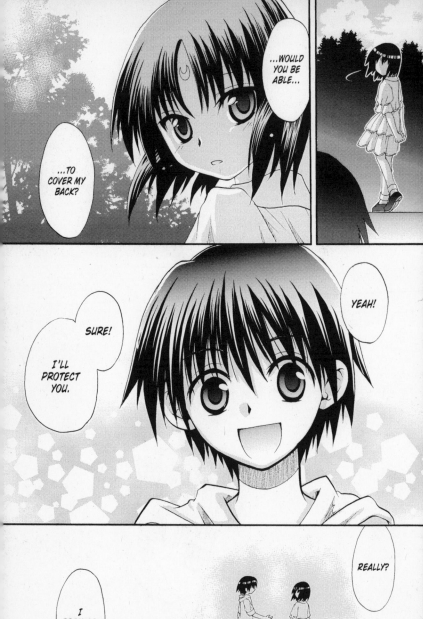
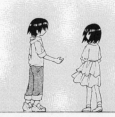

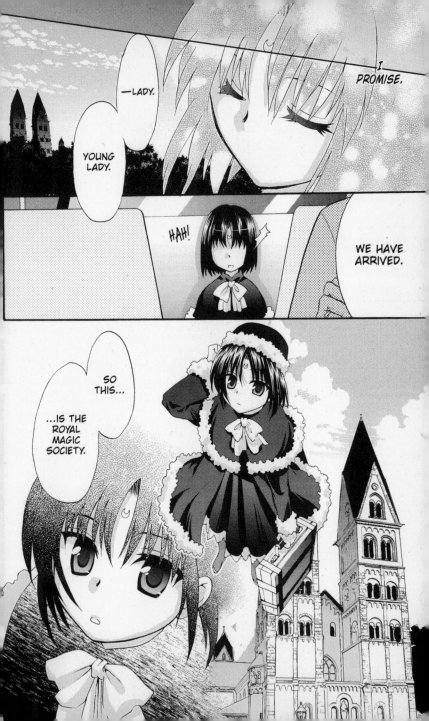

"MAGIC" ITSELF WAS INVENTED BY AND DEVELOPED IN PRIMARILY WESTERN BELIEFS, SO THERE ARE MANY WHO PERSECUTE THOSE WHO COME FROM OTHER REGIONS TO LEARN.

SINCE THE MASTERY OF MAGIC IS LARGELY DECIDED BY ONE'S HERITAGE AND TRADITIONS, IT TENDS TO BE SHROUDED IN AN AIR OF EXCLUSIVITY AND CONSERVATIVE- NESS.

A PLACE WHERE THE MOST BRILLIANT BUDDING WIZARDS FROM AROUND THE WORLD GATHER IN SEARCH OF THE "TRUE WISDOM" THAT ALL MAGIC USERS SEEK.

THE ROYAL MAGIC SOCIETY—

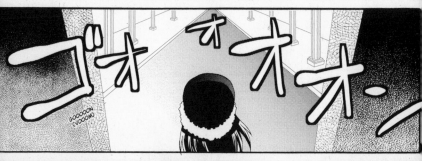

GOOOOON (VOOOM)

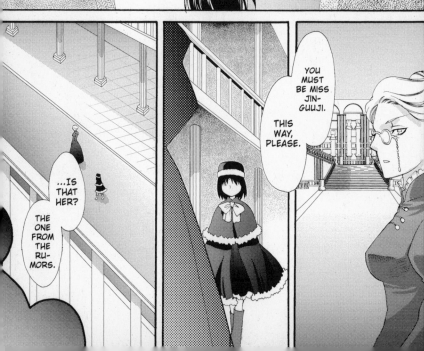

...IS THAT HER?

THE ONE FROM THE RU- MORS.

YOU MUST BE MISS JIN- GUUJI.

THIS WAY, PLEASE.

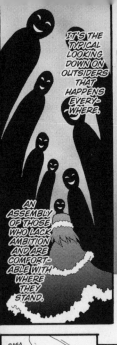

IT'S THE TYPICAL LOOKING DOWN ON OUTSIDERS THAT HAPPENS EVERY-WHERE.

AN ASSEMBLY OF THOSE WHO LACK AMBITION AND ARE COMFORT-ABLE WITH WHERE THEY STAND.

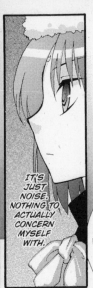

IT'S JUST NOISE. NOTHING TO ACTUALLY CONCERN MYSELF WITH.

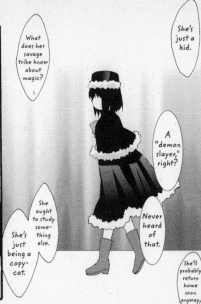

What does her savage tribe know about magic?

She's just a kid.

A "demon slayer," right?

She ought to study some-thing else.

She's just being a copy-cat.

Never heard of that.

She'll probably return home soon anyway.

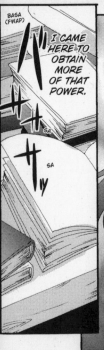

BASA (FWAP)

I CAME HERE TO OBTAIN MORE OF THAT POWER.

GA

SA

ry

...BETWEEN OUR LEVELS OF POWER.

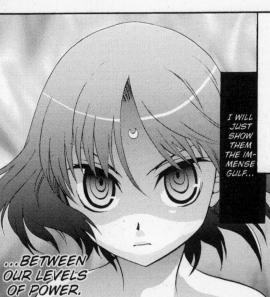

I WILL JUST SHOW THEM THE IM-MENSE GULF...

IT WILL BE EASY TO SHUT THEM UP.

KAB-
BALAH.

WIND.

THE FIVE
ELEMENTS.

FIRE.

HISTO-
RY OF
WEST-
ERN
MAGIC.

EARTH.

JAREMA.

THE
FIFTH,
ETHER.

WA-
TER.

CHAOS.

STATES
OF MAGIC
SYS-
TEMS.

—HOW
CURIOUS.

FOR THERE
BEING SO
MANY BOOKS,
THEY'RE ALL
SCIENTIFIC
BOOKS OR
HISTORY
TEXTS.

PATAN
(SHUT)

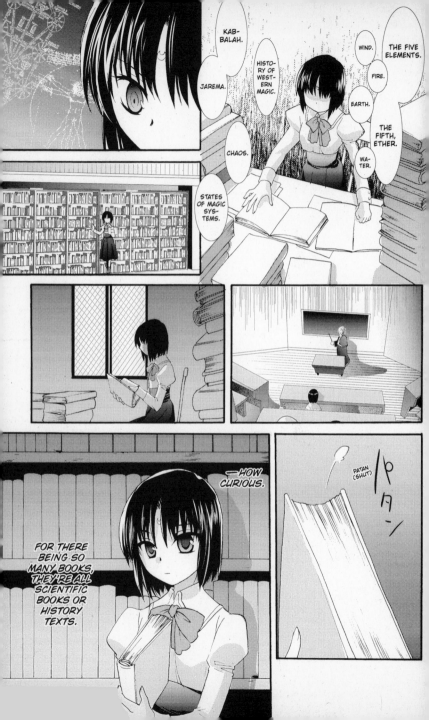

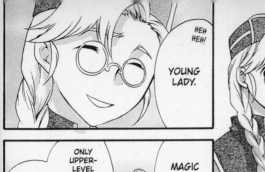

HEH HEH!

YOUNG LADY.

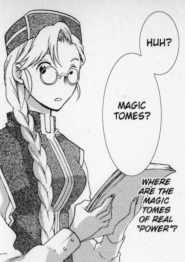

HUH?

MAGIC TOMES?

WHERE ARE THE MAGIC TOMES OF REAL "POWER"?

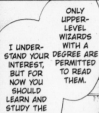

I UNDERSTAND YOUR INTEREST, BUT FOR NOW YOU SHOULD LEARN AND STUDY THE BASICS.

ONLY UPPER-LEVEL WIZARDS WITH A DEGREE ARE PERMITTED TO READ THEM.

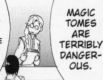

MAGIC TOMES ARE TERRIBLY DANGEROUS.

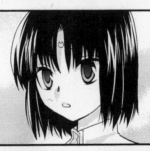

...THAT WON'T BE NECESSARY.

WOULD YOU LIKE ME TO RECOMMEND SOME OTHER GOOD TITLES TO YOU?

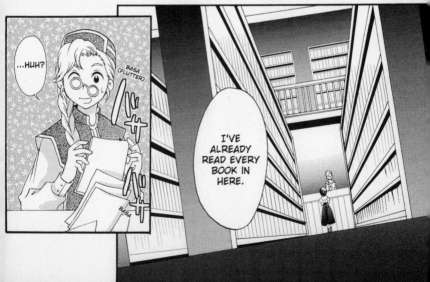

...HUH?

BASA (FLUTTER)

BASA

I'VE ALREADY READ EVERY BOOK IN HERE.

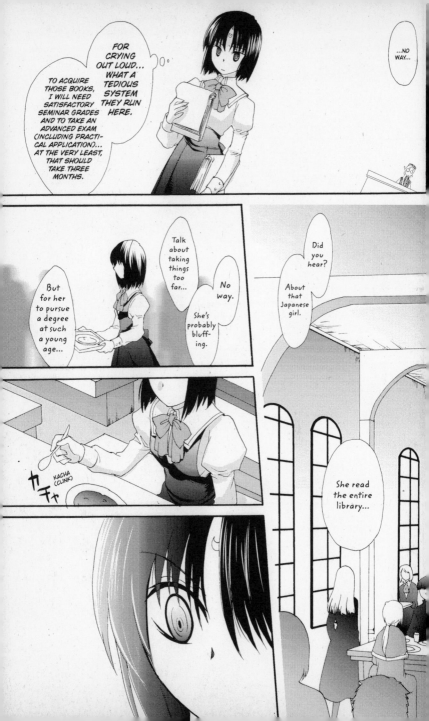

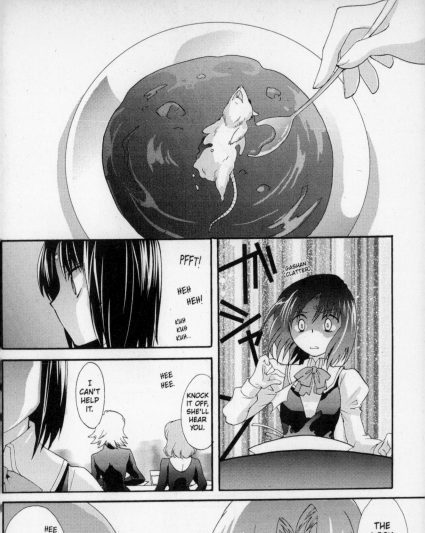

PFFT!

HEH HEH!

KUH KUH KUH...

GASHAN (CLATTER)

I CAN'T HELP IT.

HEE HEE.

KNOCK IT OFF, SHE'LL HEAR YOU.

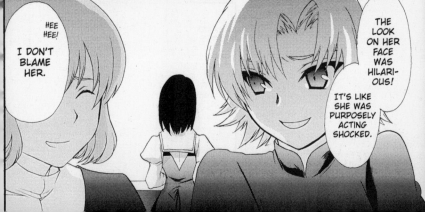

HEE HEE!

I DON'T BLAME HER.

THE LOOK ON HER FACE WAS HILARIOUS!

IT'S LIKE SHE WAS PURPOSELY ACTING SHOCKED.

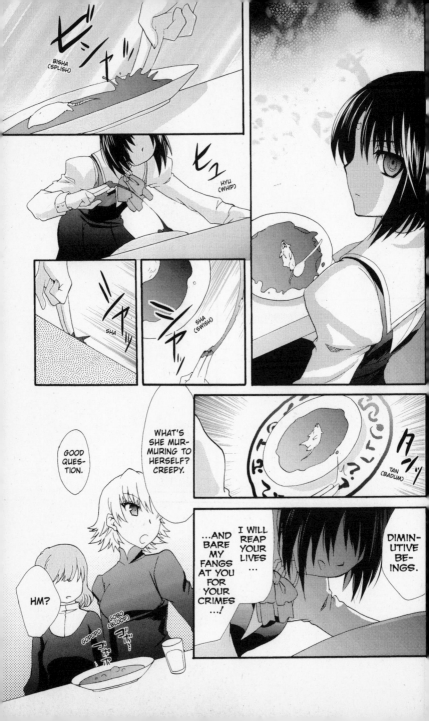

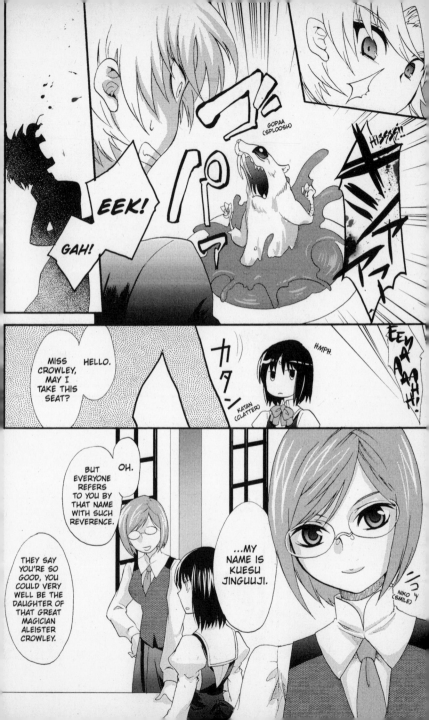

GOPAA
(SPLOOSH)

HISSSS!!...

EEK!

GAH!

MISS CROWLEY, MAY I TAKE THIS SEAT?

HELLO.

カタン
(CLATTER)

HMPH.

EEEYAAAAHH!

BUT EVERYONE REFERS TO YOU BY THAT NAME WITH SUCH REVERENCE.

OH.

THEY SAY YOU'RE SO GOOD, YOU COULD VERY WELL BE THE DAUGHTER OF THAT GREAT MAGICIAN ALEISTER CROWLEY.

...MY NAME IS KUESU JINGUUJI.

NIKO
(SMILE)

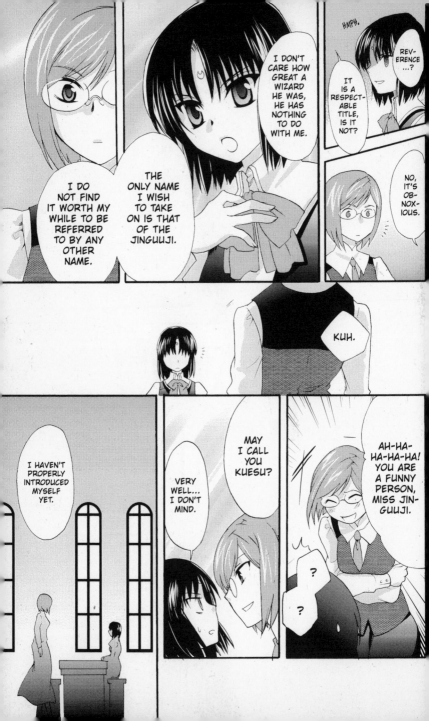

HMPH.

REVERENCE...?

IT IS A RESPECTABLE TITLE, IS IT NOT?

NO, IT'S OBNOXIOUS.

I DON'T CARE HOW GREAT A WIZARD HE WAS, HE HAS NOTHING TO DO WITH ME.

I DO NOT FIND IT WORTH MY WHILE TO BE REFERRED TO BY ANY OTHER NAME.

THE ONLY NAME I WISH TO TAKE ON IS THAT OF THE JINGUUJI.

KUH.

I HAVEN'T PROPERLY INTRODUCED MYSELF YET.

MAY I CALL YOU KUESU?

VERY WELL... I DON'T MIND.

AH-HA-HA-HA-HA! YOU ARE A FUNNY PERSON, MISS JINGUUJI.

?

?

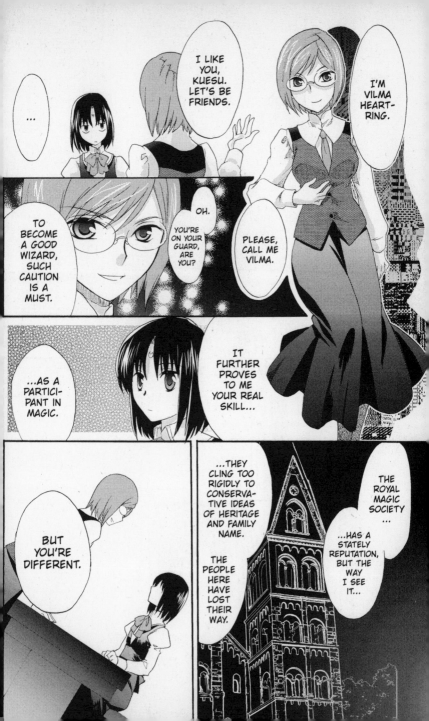

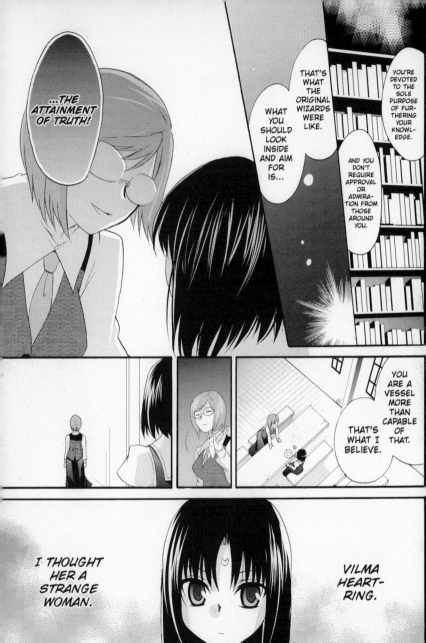

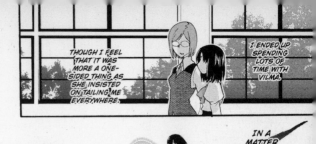

THOUGH I FEEL THAT IT WAS MORE A ONE-SIDED THING, AS SHE INSISTED ON TAILING ME EVERYWHERE.

I ENDED UP SPENDING LOTS OF TIME WITH VILMA.

AND PERFECTED MY MAGIC DAY BY DAY.

I NEVER TIRED OF IT.

IN A MATTER OF YEARS, I DEVOTED MYSELF TO THE ACQUISITION OF KNOWLEDGE.

—FOR THE JINGUUJIS—?

ALL OF IT WAS FOR THE JINGUUJI NAME.

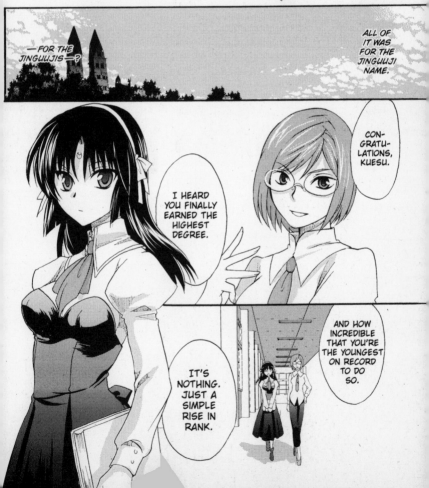

CON- GRATU- LATIONS, KUESU.

I HEARD YOU FINALLY EARNED THE HIGHEST DEGREE.

AND HOW INCREDIBLE THAT YOU'RE THE YOUNGEST ON RECORD TO DO SO.

IT'S NOTHING. JUST A SIMPLE RISE IN RANK.

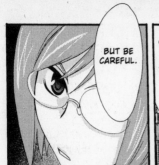 BUT BE CAREFUL.

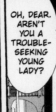 OH, DEAR. AREN'T YOU A TROUBLE-SEEKING YOUNG LADY?

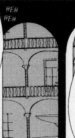 HEH HEH

IF I COULD GET ON THE BOARD AND BROWSE THE LIBRARIES FREELY, THAT WOULD BE MORE WORTH-WHILE.

EVEN WITH THE HIGHEST DEGREE, I STILL CAN'T GET MY HANDS ON THE FORBIDDEN TEXTS.

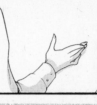 THEY HAVEN'T MADE ANY MOVES YET, BUT THIS LATEST DEVELOPMENT MAY JUST SPUR THEM INTO ACTION.

THERE'S A FACTION HERE WHO LOOKS ON YOU AS AN ENEMY.

...?

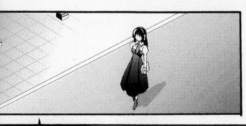 TRY NOT TO FIND YOURSELF ALONE AND KEEP YOUR WITS ABOUT YOU—

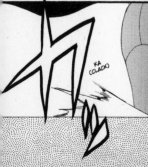

 KA (CLACK)

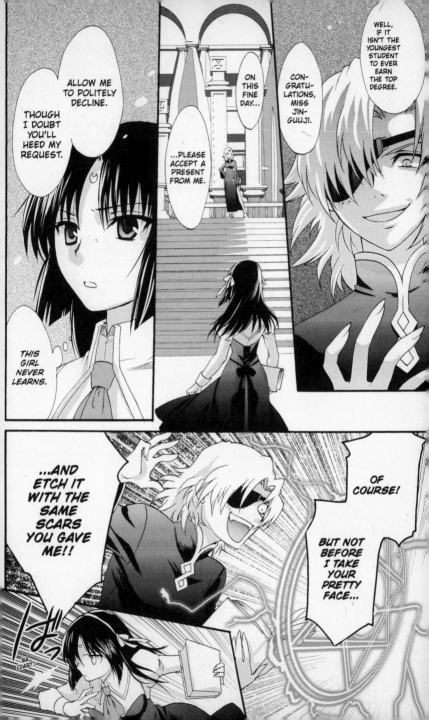

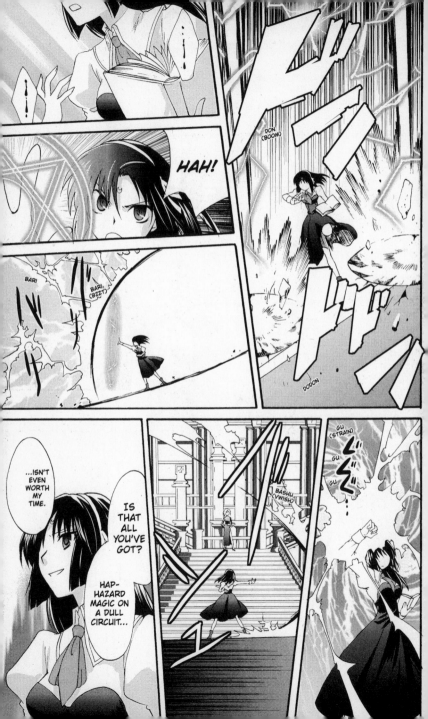

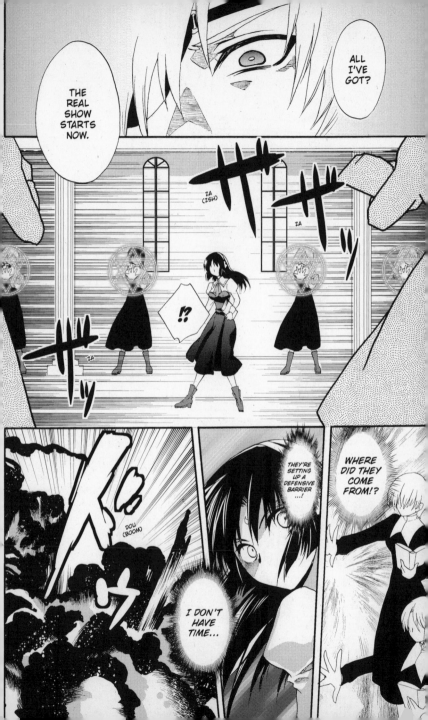

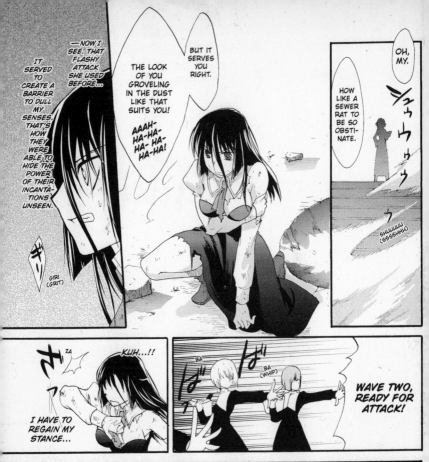

IT SERVED TO CREATE A BARRIER TO DULL MY SENSES. THAT'S HOW THEY WERE ABLE TO HIDE THE POWER OF THEIR INCANTATIONS UNSEEN.

—NOW I SEE. THAT FLASHY ATTACK SHE USED BEFORE...

THE LOOK OF YOU GROVELING IN THE DUST LIKE THAT SUITS YOU!

BUT IT SERVES YOU RIGHT.

AAAH-HA-HA-HA-HA-HA!

GIRI (GRIT)

OH, MY.

HOW LIKE A SEWER RAT TO BE SO OBSTI-NATE.

SHUUUU (SSSSHHH)

KUH...!!

I HAVE TO REGAIN MY STANCE...

ZA

BA (WHIP)

BA (WHIP)

WAVE TWO, READY FOR ATTACK!

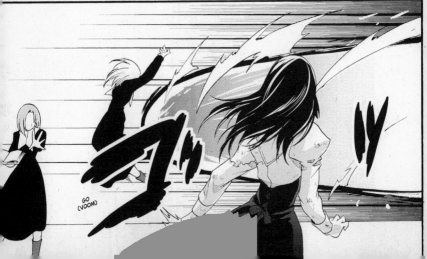

GO (VOOM)

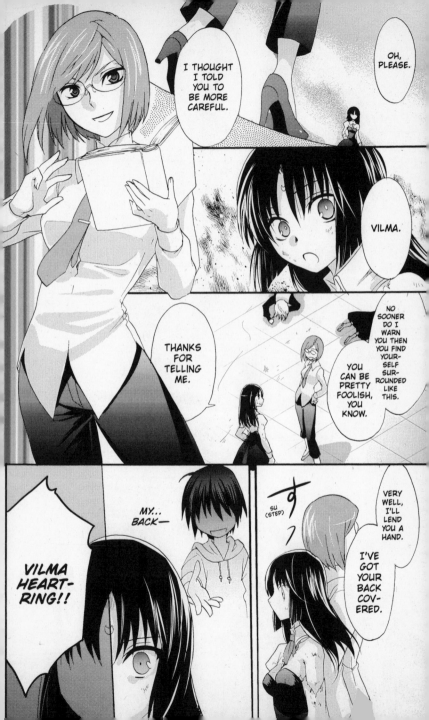

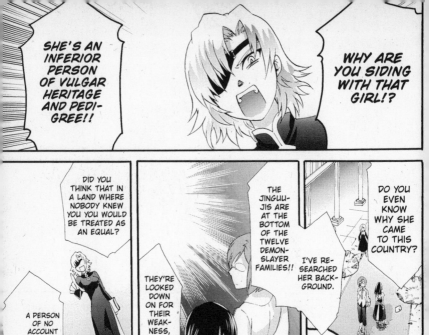

SHE'S AN INFERIOR PERSON OF VULGAR HERITAGE AND PEDI-GREE!!

WHY ARE YOU SIDING WITH THAT GIRL!?

DID YOU THINK THAT IN A LAND WHERE NOBODY KNEW YOU YOU WOULD BE TREATED AS AN EQUAL?

A PERSON OF NO ACCOUNT IS JUST THAT, NO MATTER WHERE SHE GOES.

THEY'RE LOOKED DOWN ON FOR THEIR WEAKNESS, SO SHE FLED HERE FROM HER MOTHER-LAND.

THE JINGUU-JIS ARE AT THE BOTTOM OF THE TWELVE DEMON-SLAYER FAMILIES!!

I'VE RE-SEARCHED HER BACK-GROUND.

DO YOU EVEN KNOW WHY SHE CAME TO THIS COUNTRY?

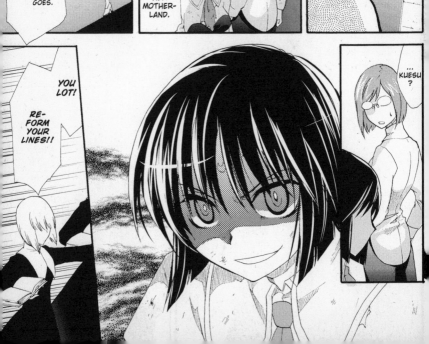

YOU LOT!

RE-FORM YOUR LINES!!

...KUESU?

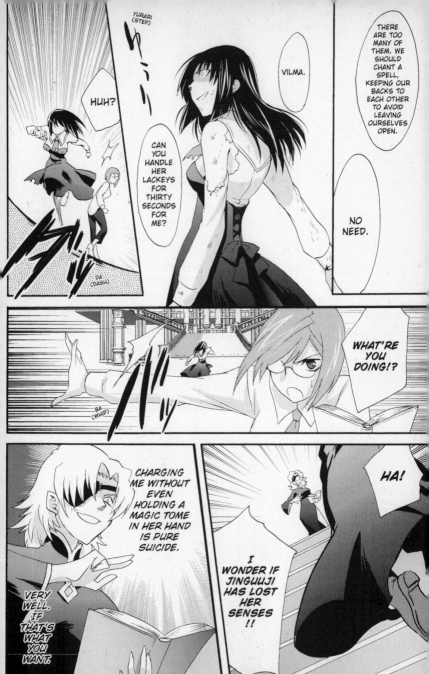

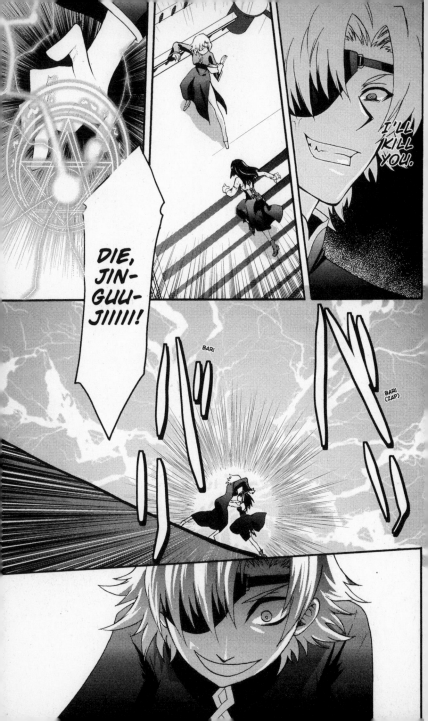

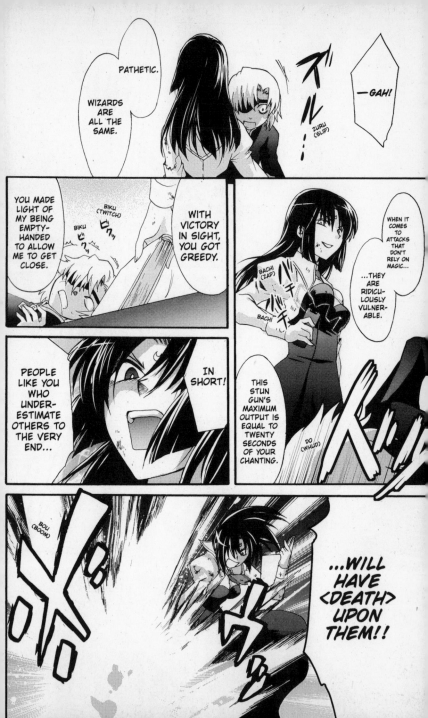

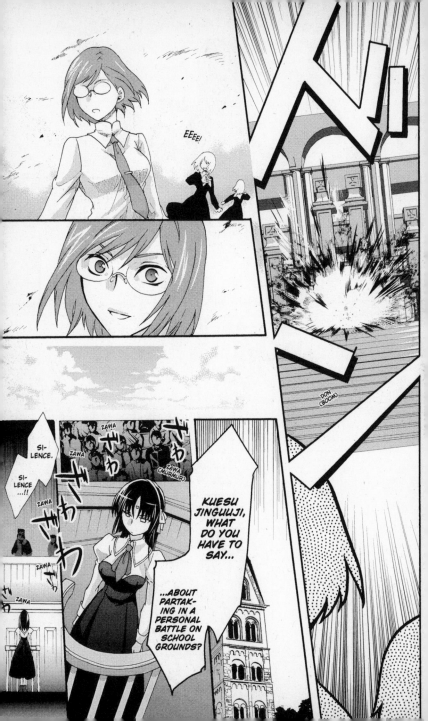

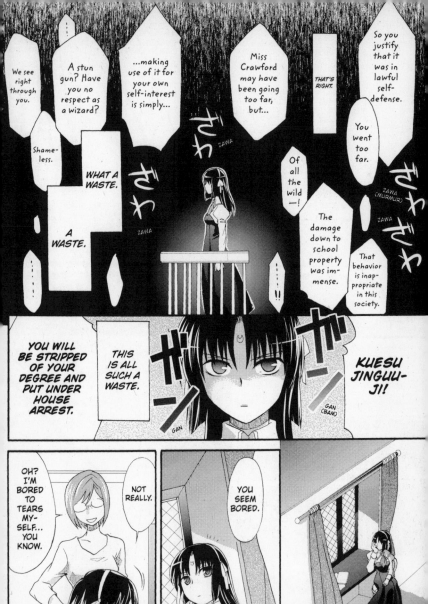

We see right through you.

A stun gun? Have you no respect as a wizard?

Shameless.

WHAT A WASTE.

A WASTE.

...making use of it for your own self-interest is simply...

Miss Crawford may have been going too far, but...

THAT'S RIGHT.

So you justify that it was in lawful self-defense.

You went too far.

Of all the wild—!

The damage down to school property was immense.

That behavior is inappropriate in this society.

ZAWA

ZAWA (MURMUR)

ZAWA

ZAWA

ZAWA

YOU WILL BE STRIPPED OF YOUR DEGREE AND PUT UNDER HOUSE ARREST.

THIS IS ALL SUCH A WASTE.

KUESU JINGUU-JI!

GAN (BAM)

GAN

OH? I'M BORED TO TEARS MY-SELF... YOU KNOW.

NOT REALLY.

YOU SEEM BORED.

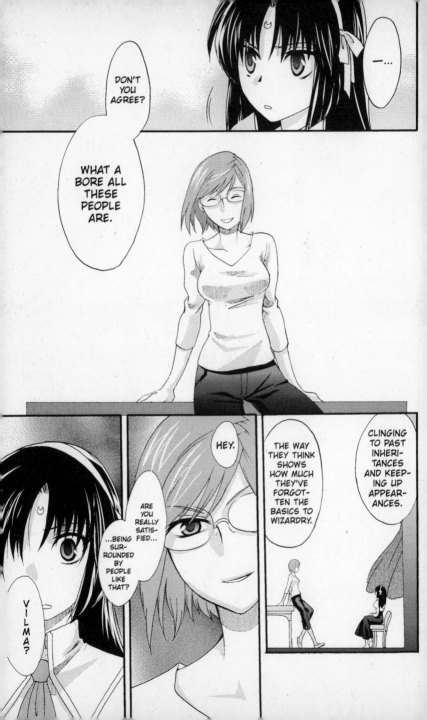

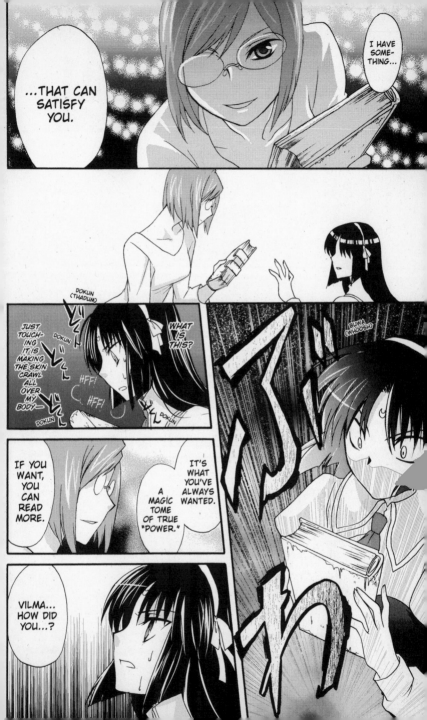

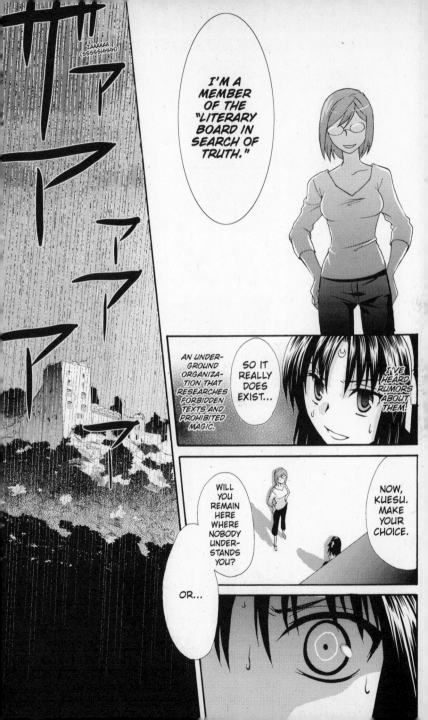

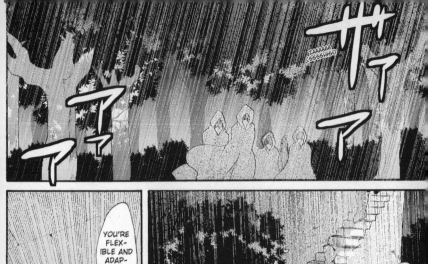

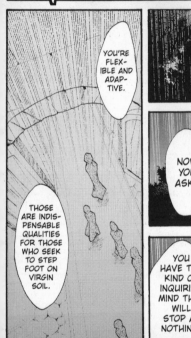

YOU'RE FLEX-IBLE AND ADAP-TIVE.

THOSE ARE INDIS-PENSABLE QUALITIES FOR THOSE WHO SEEK TO STEP FOOT ON VIRGIN SOIL.

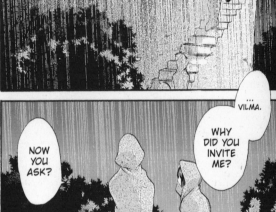

...VILMA.

WHY DID YOU INVITE ME?

NOW YOU ASK?

YOU HAVE THE KIND OF INQUIRING MIND THAT WILL STOP AT NOTHING.

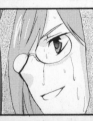

I TOLD YOU. YOU'RE CAPABLE OF ATTAIN-ING THE TRUTH.

TONIGHT IS A READING CIRCLE.

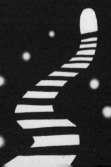

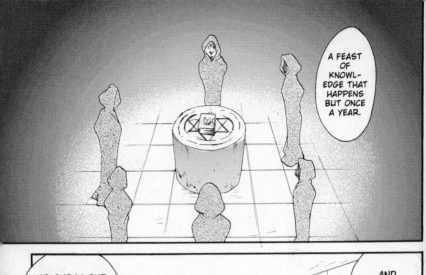

A FEAST OF KNOWL-EDGE THAT HAPPENS BUT ONCE A YEAR.

NO ONE IN OUR READING CIRCLE HAS EVER MADE CONTACT WITH THE GRIMOIRE THAT SLUMBERS IN THIS CASTLE AND MADE IT BACK SAFELY.

AND THE TEXT THIS TIME WILL BE A DIFFICULT ONE TO DEAL WITH.

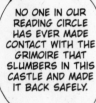

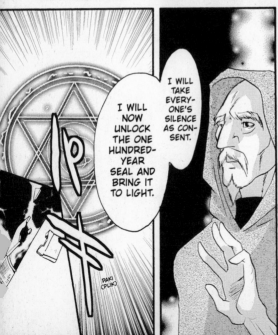

I WILL TAKE EVERY-ONE'S SILENCE AS CON-SENT.

I WILL NOW UNLOCK THE ONE HUNDRED-YEAR SEAL AND BRING IT TO LIGHT.

PAKI (PLIK)

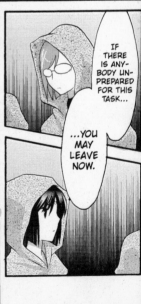

IF THERE IS ANY-BODY UN-PREPARED FOR THIS TASK...

...YOU MAY LEAVE NOW.

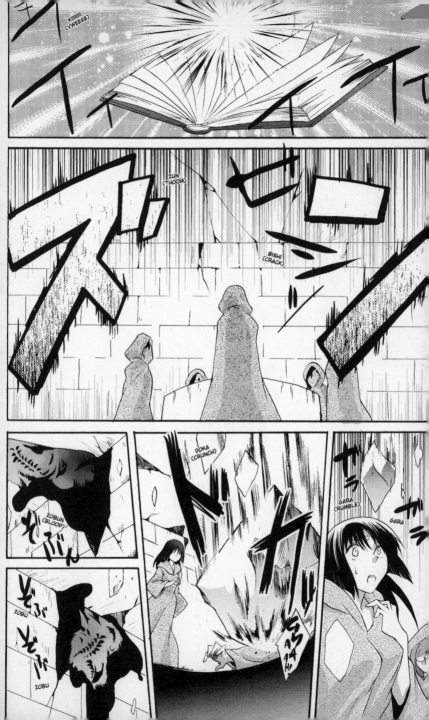

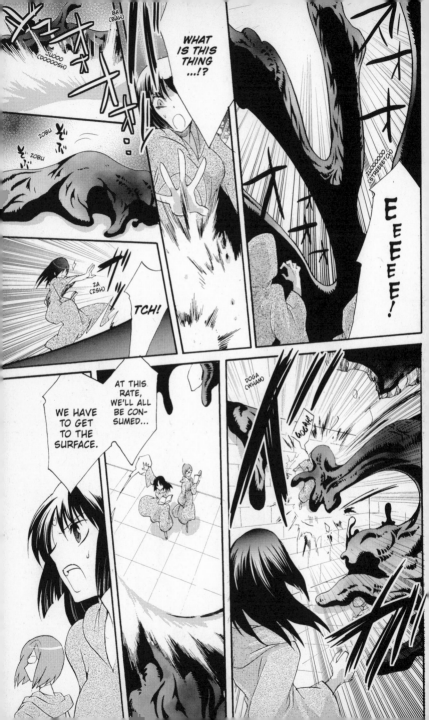

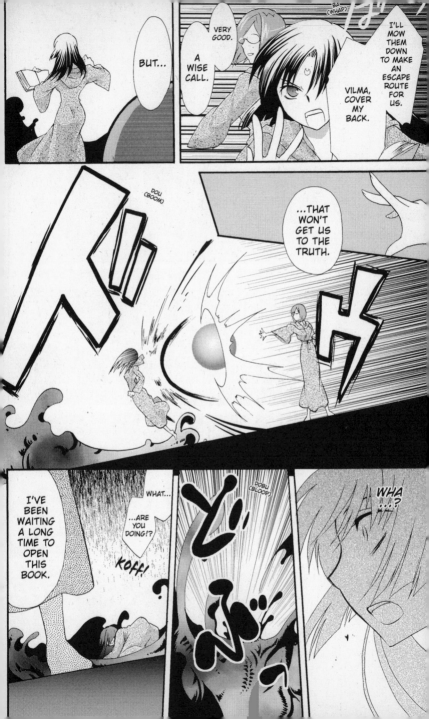

GA
(GRAB)

THIS TORRENT OF MUD IS A SEA OF KNOWLEDGE THAT HAS OVERFLOWED FROM THE MAGIC TEXT.

BUT...

ONLY THOSE WHO CAN ENDURE ITS MASSIVE AMOUNT OF INFORMATION AND STAY AFLOAT WILL ARRIVE AT THE TRUTH.

...EVERYONE WHO HAS COME IN DIRECT CONTACT WITH THE TRUTH HAS GONE INSANE.

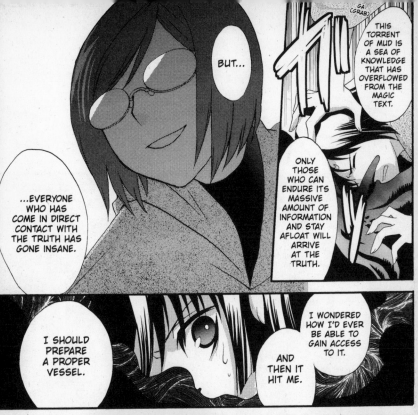

I WONDERED HOW I'D EVER BE ABLE TO GAIN ACCESS TO IT.

I SHOULD PREPARE A PROPER VESSEL.

AND THEN IT HIT ME.

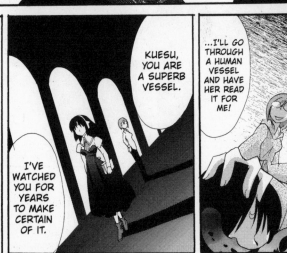

KUESU, YOU ARE A SUPERB VESSEL.

...I'LL GO THROUGH A HUMAN VESSEL AND HAVE HER READ IT FOR ME!

IF I CAN'T COME IN DIRECT CONTACT...

AND SO...

I'VE WATCHED YOU FOR YEARS TO MAKE CERTAIN OF IT.

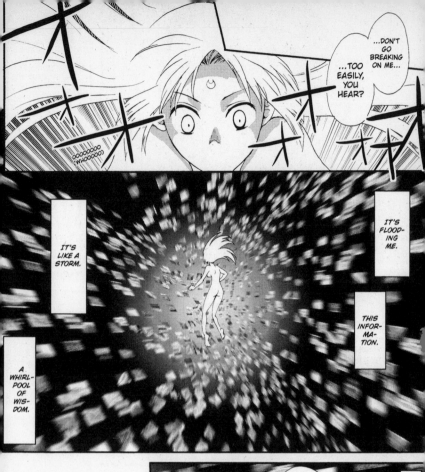

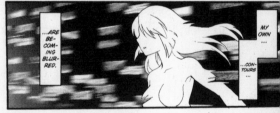

AND YET I FEEL COMFORTABLE.

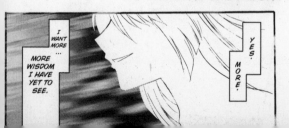

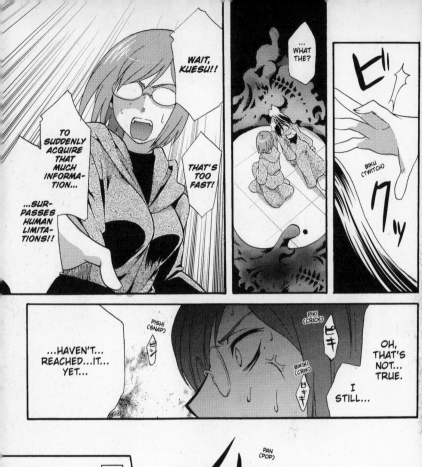

WAIT, KUESU!!

TO SUDDENLY ACQUIRE THAT MUCH INFORMATION...

...SUR-PASSES HUMAN LIMITA-TIONS!!

THAT'S TOO FAST!

...WHAT THE?

BIKU (TWITCH)

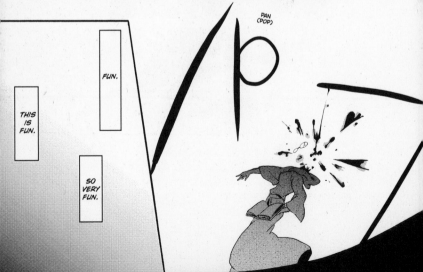

PISHI (SNAP)

PIKI (CRICK)

BIKIKI (CRIK)

...HAVEN'T... REACHED...IT... YET...

OH, THAT'S NOT... TRUE.

I STILL...

PAN (POP)

THIS IS FUN.

FUN.

SO VERY FUN.

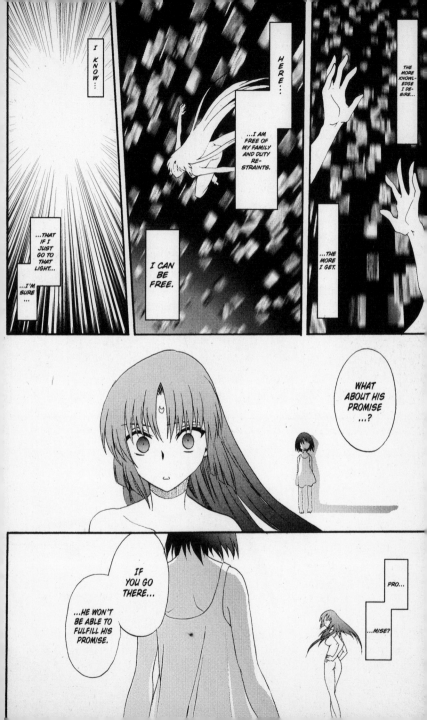

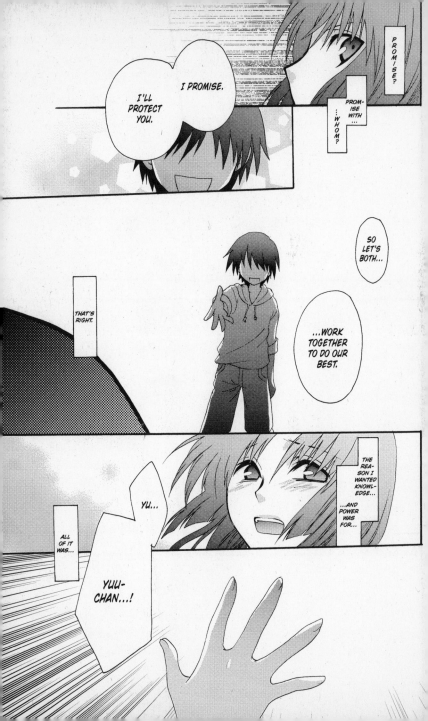

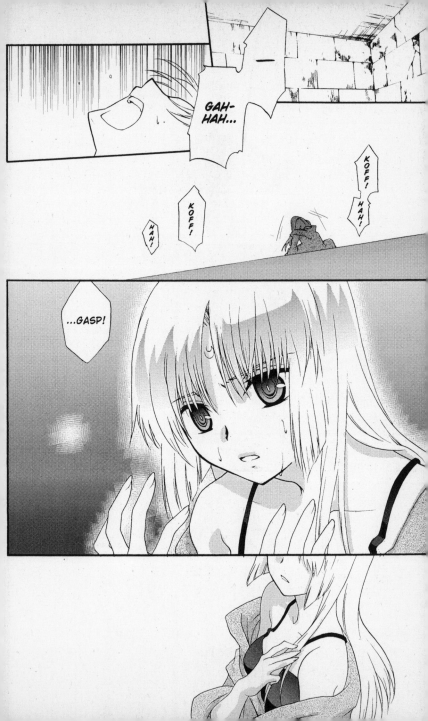

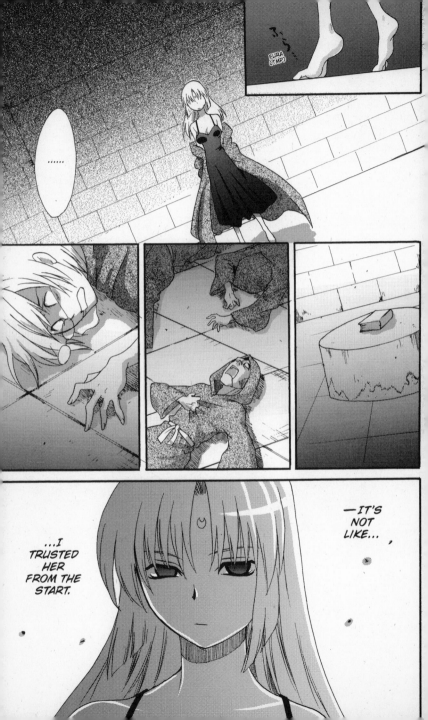

FURA
(TMP)

......

...I TRUSTED HER FROM THE START.

—IT'S NOT LIKE... ,

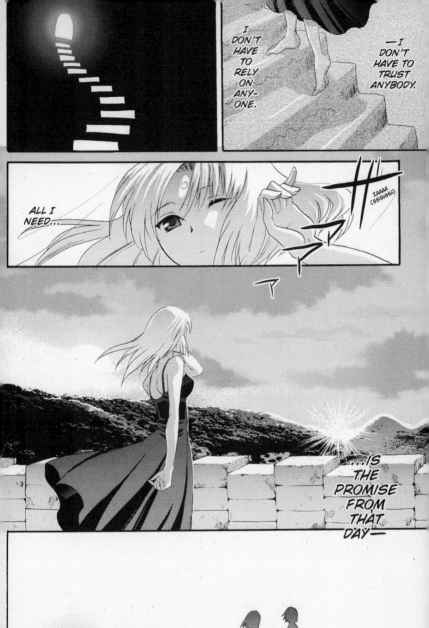

THE END

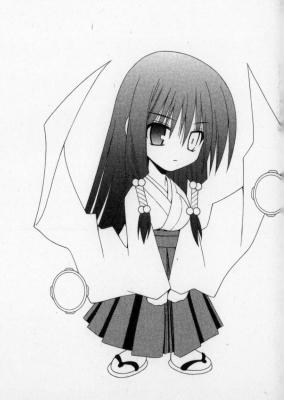

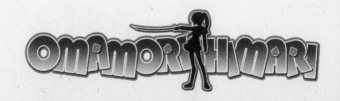

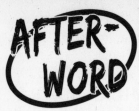

AFTER-WORD

MILAN MATRA

ACTUALLY THESE *OMAMORI HIMARI* PAST STORIES AND SPIN-OFFS HAD ALWAYS BEEN PLANNED TO BE RELEASED AS A SHORT PUBLICATION, BUT ALL OF A SUDDEN, THE PLAN FOR THEM TO BE COMPILED INTO A VOLUME BECAUSE THERE WASN'T ENOUGH TIME TO DO THEM SEPARATELY CAME UP, AND THAT IS HOW I FOUND MYSELF WITH MY FIRST ANTHOLOGY EVER. STARTING WITH MIKAZUKI-SENSEI, I SO, SO, SO APPRECIATE HAVING GOTTEN TO WORK WITH KUROHACHI-SAN, SHINSHIN-SAN, NIKUBANARE-SAN, AND YAMAMOTO-SAN. AND TO ALL YOU READERS OUT THERE, PLEASE KEEP FOLLOWING *OMAMORI HIMARI* HEREAFTER TOO!

KOUGETSU MIKAZUKI

HI, IT'S ME, KOUGETSU MIKAZUKI. I CAN'T BELIEVE *OMAMORI HIMARI*, VOLUME 0, IS FINALLY COMING TO FRUITION! OH, HAPPY DAY! ♪ BECAUSE IT WAS VOLUME 0, I WROTE THE STORY A LITTLE DIFFERENTLY FROM THE USUAL NOVEL. IT WAS A SHORT FLASHBACK STORY MADE UP OF MEMORIES. IT TELLS OF ROUGH-AND-TOUGH RINKO AND EMOTIONLESS, EXPRESSIONLESS YUUTO (CAUSED BY HIS CHARM). RINKO'S ALWAYS BEING CALLED A FLAT-CHESTED COMMONER AND GETTING THE SHORT END OF THE STICK FOR JUST BEING THE CHILD-HOOD FRIEND, BUT SHE REALLY IS A GOOD GIRL! I TRIED TO COMMUNICATE TO YOU ALL RINKO'S CLUMSY WAY OF EXPRESSING HER VULNER-ABLE GIRLY SIDE.

NIKUBANARE

I RECENTLY GOT A TUMOR IN MY NIPPLE. IT HAPPENS TO BOYS IN THEIR ADOLESCENCE. BUT THIS IS THE THIRD TIME IT'S HAPPENED TO ME. I THOUGHT FOR SURE IT MEANT THAT I'D FALLEN EVEN MORE IN LOVE WITH MY GIRL, SO I TOLD HER: "IT SEEMS I'VE FALLEN FOR YOU AGAIN." TO WHICH SHE VAGUELY WAVED HER HAND TO WARD OFF THAT OLD MAN SMELL AND SIMPLY CONTINUED TO STARE AT ME WITH MOIST EYES.

SHINSHIN

HELLO AND NICE TO MEET YOU. MY NAME IS SHINSHIN. I'M VERY HAPPY TO HAVE GOT-TEN TO WORK ON SUCH A FANTASTIC TITLE AS *OMAMORI HIMARI*. I HOPE YOU ALL ENJOYED IT TOO. THANK YOU VERY MUCH.

KUROHACHI

KUESU IS MY ALL-TIME FAVORITE HEROINE, SO I WAS HAPPY TO HAVE GOTTEN TO DRAW A STORY ABOUT HER.

ILLUSTRATION: MILAN MATRA

OMAMORI HIMARI 0

MILAN MATRA
KOUGETSU MIKAZUKI
NIKUBANARE
SHINSHIN
KUROHACHI

Translation: Christine Dashiell • Lettering: Alice Baker

OMAMORI HIMARI 0
© 2009 MATRA MILAN • MIKAZUKI KOUGETSU • NIKUBANARE • SHINSHIN • KUROHACHI.
© 2009 Miran Matora / Fujimishobou / Omahima Partners. First published in Japan in 2009 by FUJIMISHOBO CO., LTD., Tokyo. English translation rights arranged with KADOKAWA SHOTEN Co., Ltd., Tokyo through TUTTLE-MORI AGENCY, INC., Tokyo.

Translation © 2012 by Hachette Book Group, Inc.

Yen Press
Hachette Book Group
237 Park Avenue, New York, NY 10017

www.HachetteBookGroup.com
www.YenPress.com

Yen Press is an imprint of Hachette Book Group, Inc. The Yen Press name and logo are trademarks of Hachette Book Group, Inc.

First Yen Press Edition: September 2012

ISBN: 978-0-316-20941-0

10 9 8 7 6 5 4 3 2 1

BVG

Printed in the United States of America

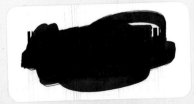